WHAT EVERY STUDENT SHOULD KNOW ABOUT RESEARCHING ONLINE

Second Edition

Dave Munger

Shireen Campbell
Davidson College

PEARSON

Boston Columbus Indianapolis New York San Francisco Upper Saddle River
Amsterdam Cape Town Dubai London Madrid Milan Munich Paris Montreal Toronto
Delhi Mexico City Sao Paulo Sydney Hong Kong Seoul Singapore Taipei Tokyo

Executive Editor: Lynn Huddon
Director of Marketing: Megan Galvin-Fak
Development Editor: Paul Sarkis
Senior Supplements Editor: Donna Campion
Project Coordination, Text Design, and Electronic Page Makeup: Grapevine Publishing
    Services, Inc.
Cover Designer: Alison Barth Burgoyne
Senior Manufacturing Buyer: Roy Pickering
Printer and Binder: Courier Westford

Copyright © 2012, 2007 Pearson Education, Inc.

Please visit us at www.pearsonhighered.com

5 17

www.pearsonhighered.com

ISBN 13: 978-0-205-85646-6
ISBN 10:   0-205-85646-2

CONTENTS

PREFACE

Why should anyone need a book about researching online any more? Between smartphones and Wi-Fi hot spots, college students are able to be online 24/7, probably wherever they are. We routinely Google and tweet. We post "happy birthday" messages via social networking and tag photos of friends and family.

If familiarity with Facebook and Google were all it took to master searching for high-quality information, then today's college students would have it made. Unfortunately, while even elementary school students are taught how to open a browser and type in a search query, finding *reliable* information, written by experts, remains as elusive as ever. Students must negotiate around biased sources, uninformed sources, and advertisements, plus cope with the overwhelming mass of information available.

What Every Student Should Know About Researching Online starts with what everyone knows about online research and then moves beyond that, showing students how to utilize the Internet's tremendous malleability and interactivity to find reliable, informed information on just about anything. We begin by showing students that the challenges of beginning research projects can be mitigated with effective use of the Internet to narrow possible topics. Next, we describe the vast array of online resources for searching and discuss how Google and *Wikipedia* may be useful places to start, but other resources such as Project Gutenberg and Google Scholar can be more effective for finding acceptable sources for college research. Finally, we provide students with tips on how to filter through the massive amount of information available and evaluate potential sources for credibility and reliability, as well as how to manage their information and integrate sources effectively into arguments with appropriate citation.

While *What Every Student Should Know About Researching Online* is based on our 2006 edition of the same title, it has been extensively revised to reflect both the widespread changes that have taken place online in the intervening six years, and the latest findings on student online research practices. Today's web is dominated by interactive sites such as Facebook and *Wikipedia*, where millions of users participate in a constantly changing community. Commonly known as Web 2.0, the Internet has awesome power, with tweets and blogs disseminating information almost instantly. However, it can also be divisive, with narrowly partisan viewpoints and angry rejoinders spread as readily as more nuanced and complex analysis.

We show students how to use this powerful community to help locate reliable information that meets the requirements of their assignments.

This book has been designed to be the most useful tool possible for anyone doing online research. Specialized vocabulary is **bold and underlined** to alert readers to terms defined in the glossary, and additional terms are defined there as well. Text that users must input is displayed in a `special typeface` to make it easy to recognize. URLs are displayed in ***bold italic*** and without confusing angle brackets. Most importantly, critical concepts are both explained in the text and reinforced visually with real-world examples. We think it's an indispensable guide for negotiating what has become an increasingly powerful resource, but one whose power is at the mercy of its users.

Acknowledgments

Thanks to Greta, Jim, Nora, Jeremy, Jonathan, and Alistair, who were both patient and accommodating as we worked feverishly to meet deadline on this project. Thanks, too, to Paul Sarkis and Lynn Huddon at Pearson Education for their valuable suggestions for this revision, to the project coordinator, Dianne Hall, and to the copy editor and proofreader, Leslie Ballard.

1

Developing a
Research Focus

Like most college students, you use the Internet for personal research, doing searches on everything from when a new movie is showing in 3-D to investigating where you should apply for a summer internship. You probably begin this type of research with a clear sense of what topic interests you and what you need to learn about it. You also know how to narrow your topic, depending on what you find. For example, perhaps you heard that a regional newspaper has a summer internship program. When you investigate on the newspaper website, you realize that the paper offers several different internships; now you need to figure out which internship or internships you want and which positions match your background experience. According to an extensive recent study, *Truth Be Told: How College Students Evaluate and Use Information in the Digital Age*, college students have little difficulty in the beginning stages of personal research. They begin with the questions they need to answer and continue to refine these questions as they learn more. In contrast, nearly 85 percent of the students reported that getting started on academic research for classes was the hardest part of the process. Many also found it difficult to define a topic and narrow it down.

In this chapter, we consider why starting an academic research project can be a struggle and discuss how to use skills you already have to make your research experience successful.

Clarify the purpose of research assignments

As you know, the amount of information available on the Internet can be overwhelming, making it difficult to begin the research process. Sometimes students fear that a topic will not meet the professor's expectations, which can lead to a fear of commitment. Sometimes it isn't a fear of beginning, but a misunderstanding of the research process and purpose that gets in the way. We have also encountered students who believe that they are supposed to read everything available on a subject until they know the two main sides, then pick the "right" side to support—the one that will most please the instructor—and then support that side with the "right" number of sources. Confronted with the wealth of information available online, students can become frustrated and confused.

Consider the situation of Jasmine, a student in a freshman writing seminar titled "Democracy Today." She has been assigned a research project and knows that her instructor seems quite interested in the topic of political polarization. Her textbook covers the topic briefly, but does not mention any additional resources. So, Jasmine begins in the way she always begins research, using the **search engine** Google to investigate the term "political polarization." (We define and discuss various kinds of search engines in chapter 2.) In seconds, her initial search yields 3,250,000 hits (see figure 1.1). Jasmine's initial results range from a *Wikipedia* entry on the concept of political polarization to multiple related news items and commentary, plus a book-length study on polarization in American politics.

Reading everything she found would be impossible. After reading the *Wikipedia* entry, Jasmine realizes that experts debate both the causes and the effects of polarization and even disagree about whether polarization is good or bad. Another one of her top hits distinguishes between *elite polarization* and *mass polarization,* terms she doesn't know. Rather than exploring a hot topic with two clear sides, she has selected a topic with many possible subtopics and approaches.

At this point, some students might quit and begin hunting for another topic that seems more clear-cut. Yet, the purpose of research projects is to encourage students to get curious, to learn how to tunnel into a topic and come up with interesting questions that will lead to further discovery, and, ultimately, an arguable thesis.

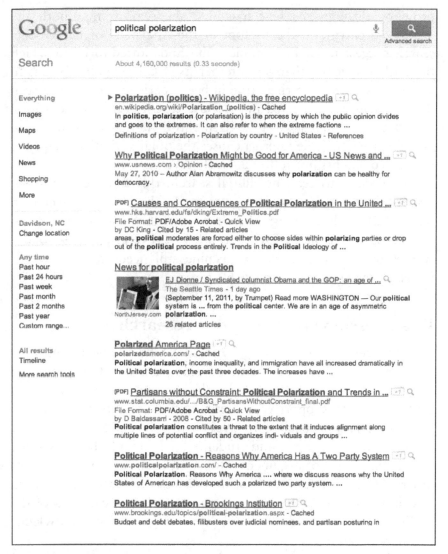

Figure 1.1: Google search on political polarization

Narrow your topic through pre-research

To succeed in a research project, you have to develop a good process for moving from broad topics to narrow topics, which you stand a better chance of exploring in full. The Internet can aid in this process. Let's return to the example of Jasmine, who's interested in political polarization. When she spends a bit of time prowling through the first few hits, she realizes that both the *Wikipedia* entry and the bottom of the first page of her Google search suggest possible subtopics. She finds an editorial in which the author suggests that the Internet itself causes polarization. In some ways, this claim rings true in her experience, as she has seen that the comments posted in response to editorials in the school newspaper are almost always extreme in their views. But how can anyone prove that the Internet causes the polarization? Perhaps the ranting comments just reflect a deeply divided society.

She decides to redo her initial search, this time searching for "political polarization and the Internet." The results (depicted in figure 1.2) are heartening: More than a million hits are recorded, but she sees that the first result is a list of several recent scholarly studies on the subject. While Jasmine still needs to narrow her focus, she's closer to a manageable topic.

Use questions to drive your research

Many students come to college with well-developed—and in some cases teacher-prescribed—routines for research. One common approach is to make up your mind about a topic, write your thesis, find research to support your thesis, outline your paper, and then write it. This approach may work well when a class has spent weeks studying a topic, and students have already been exposed to the main lines of argument. However, such an approach strips any real discovery from the research process, for reading merely to find information that confirms a point of view cheats you of the ability to let your ideas evolve as you gain more knowledge through research.

Rather than begin with a thesis and try to prove it, we recommend approaching research with a question or questions to be answered or refined. In considering the Internet and political polarization, for example, you could approach this topic with a number of different questions in mind, depending on your interests and class requirements. Perhaps you enjoy history and are interested in to what extent political polarization has become more intense since the advent of the Internet. In this case, your question might be, Are American politics more polarized before or after the advent of the

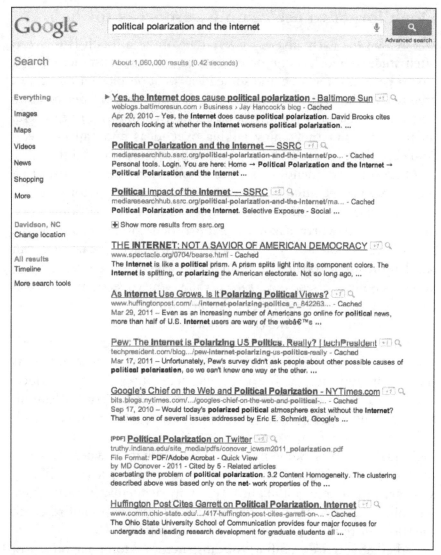

Figure 1.2: Google search for political polarization and the Internet

web? The question could be improved if you applied some limits to develop a clear point of comparison, such as selecting two decades to compare.

In the end, you may not have a clear answer to your question, for the answer may depend on who is asking and how. But you would be better able to weigh all the perspectives you find on the question and make up your own mind.

Don't forget to use campus resources for help

One reason the early phases of research can be difficult is that too often students work alone or hesitate to ask for assistance. If you have a general topic area and some ideas of subtopics within it, but aren't sure what you want to explore, you should consider meeting with a tutor at your writing support service. Tutors won't be experts on the topic, but they enjoy talking over ideas and can help you come up with some relevant questions about a topic or subtopic.

Once you have identified several possible questions relevant to a topic area, we recommend speaking with your instructor to see if he or she has any additional recommendations. A question can be important and worth asking, yet too broad for the scope of the assignment or outside the scope of the class. In such a case, you can wind up reading too much and writing a generalized report that argues nothing effectively. Or, perhaps the question has been explored thoroughly in the professional literature already, leaving you no room to add to the conversation.

While *Truth Be Told*, the survey on student research experiences, shows that students routinely consult their instructors as they craft and pursue research questions, they often overlook another valuable campus resource: the trained library professionals, who know the variety of powerful electronic resources available that can sift through masses of information and return high-quality results. Sometimes, because of when or where students do their work, they do not work with library staff. (Few library staff are available at midnight.) Yet many academic libraries have an online help feature through which students can email research questions or request one-on-one appointments.

Whether you are emailing your instructor or someone on a professional staff, such as a librarian, take a little care in crafting your message. Begin with a clear subject header that indicates what you are asking, such as: "Research help for Eng. 110 essay on Hamlet and madness." When a reference librarian is wading through multiple electronic requests for help in locating specific resources, whose email is she going to take more seriously? A clear, concise one, such as:

> Mrs. Franklin, I am interested in psychoanalytic approaches to Hamlet's madness in Shakespeare's play. I have found good criticism in MLA, but need help understanding some basic psychological terminology. Can you please suggest a good general resource?

Or, the one that reads:

> Cnt find gd info o/madness in Shks Ham. Cld I mt w/y at 2200? fwiw, hv ch w/MLA.

In the first case, the reference librarian knows where the student has looked and what he or she needs help with. In the second, the student's needs aren't clear, and the abbreviations and tone suggest a less prepared, perhaps unreasonably demanding student, who no one would look forward to helping.

You will also receive more effective assistance if you are specific about where and how you've looked so far, as illustrated in the sample email given. By *where*, we mean which resources you've consulted, and by *how*, we mean what search terms you've used. If you keep track of this information and explain your process, the library staff or professor won't waste time giving you unnecessary advice.

2

FINDING THE
RIGHT INFORMATION

When you begin a research project, you should use strategies appropriate to the course and assignment as you search for sources. If you are required to submit a research proposal on a topic, your search will begin perhaps weeks earlier, as you search for potential topics and information. If your instructor assigns your topic area, you will start searching within the parameters of the topic. However, as you begin your search, be prepared for the unexpected: Research always proceeds with smooth and rough patches, as not all sources pan out. Other sources may offer information that takes your project in unanticipated directions. Successful students develop a method for the research process that begins with general searches and sources, then becomes more specific as the topic and focus narrow.

In this chapter, we describe how to use a range of electronic materials to get the information you need. We first cover how to conduct general searches to get background information on a topic. Following these general search tips, we discuss how to draw from a wide variety of more specialized search strategies in order to locate the most useful sources for your project.

Searching with general sources

Using your library website

Almost all major learning institutions have searchable indexes of their holdings on the web. If you don't find what you need on your own library's site, try searching the catalogs from other institutions. You can request holdings from other schools via your own library's interlibrary loan department.

Beyond giving you location information for relevant books, videos, and government documents, your school's site may give you access to additional resources available only to students and faculty, such as searchable indexes like *The Readers Guide to Periodical Literature* or searchable encyclopedias like the *Encyclopedia Britannica.* If your library does not have such a resource or you are not on campus and cannot access the school website, you may still be able to access some encyclopedic resources electronically. Most major encyclopedias now offer a full information service online—for a subscription fee. One notable exception can be found at *www.bartleby.com,* where, for example, you can search a full edition of *The World Fact Book* for free.

Your library has a vast array of materials, and as many ways to search for them. Most of what you will find comes from **scholarly databases**. For example, PsychInfo can be used to search resources about psychology, many of which are not available on the free Internet. Web of Knowledge covers an even wider array of sources and uncovers connections between them in ways that a general web search cannot. Nothing beats setting up a session with a reference librarian to learn more about how to use the wealth of resources in your library.

Searching on the web

Whenever you use a web browser, you will be pointed to a **search engine** or **subject directory**. With a subject directory, you search for sites by selecting from lists of subjects. Gradually, you narrow the subject lists to the topic that interests you. With a search engine, you can type a word or set of words, and it will present you with a list of sites where that word appears.

While it may be convenient to perform your search with whichever search tool comes up when you load your browser, be aware that you have many more options. The only reason you see the search tool you do is because that search tool company has a paid agreement with the company that makes your browser. Identify the search tool that works best for the type of resources you need. To learn more about subject directories, see pages 19–21. For more on search engines, see "Searching with web search engines."

Searching with web search engines

Where do you go when you want to find information on the Internet? If you're like most people, you just type your question in the search bar of your computer's web browser or your mobile phone. Then a list of answers comes up, and you click on them one by one until you are satisfied. This can be a powerful way of answering simple factual questions like, Who is the lead singer of the Red Hot Chili Peppers? This strategy is so easy and effective that it's tempting to use it for nearly any question you have.

You can and should use similar strategies when you move beyond simple questions to the complex ones you ask when you work on an academic research project. But in order to make the most of the Internet's power, you need to know exactly what your computer is doing to provide you with these quick answers. You probably know it's relying on a search engine like Google or Bing, but you may not have questioned how these sites find the information you need.

Search engines don't themselves contain much information; instead, they automate the process of searching the entire web—and increasingly, they go beyond the web to uncover the deep information stored in databases and other systems connected to the Internet. They find this information by using robots, programs that automatically visit and catalog all the information they encounter. They then use sophisticated **algorithms** to try and match the words you've typed in your search phrase with the information they have indexed.

If you're starting a project about the play *Hamlet* by William Shakespeare, you might begin by typing `Hamlet` in your search bar. Depending on your computer and browser, your results will usually be displayed by either Google (*google.com*) or Bing (*bing.com*). Figure 2.1 shows the search results for `Hamlet` from Google and Bing. The results are similar: Both sites produce "about" ten million results, and both link first to the *Wikipedia* page on *Hamlet*. Both link to the Internet Movie Database (IMDB, *imdb.com*) pages for the 1998 film version of *Hamlet*, and to vari-

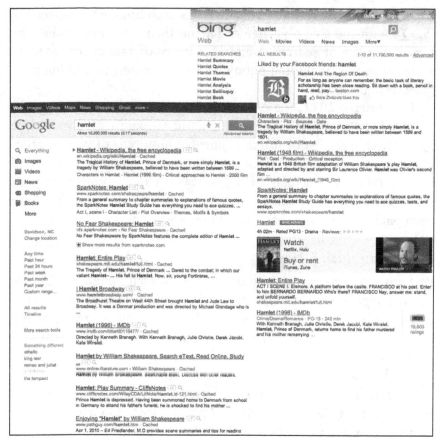

Figure 2.1: Searching for "Hamlet" using Google and Bing

ous "notes" for *Hamlet* offered for purchase, as well as free and paid movies, and a searchable version of the play's text. While many of these sites may come in handy, you'll need to select more keywords to narrow your search.

One word of caution regarding searching with most commercial Internet search engines: Because they are for-profit enterprises, search engines and other websites constantly seek new ways to make money. One obvious way search engines do this is through advertising. It's easy to avoid banner ads if you're not interested, but other ads may not be as easy to dodge. For example, the Bing search results displayed here include options to buy or rent film versions of *Hamlet* embedded within the search. In addition, commercial websites know that most readers reach their sites via search engines, so they have staff dedicated to Search Engine Optimization (**SEO**), with the sole objective of having their site appear near the top of the list of search results. A variety of tactics are used to accomplish this, including phony websites devoted to making their page seem popular.

In February 2011, the *New York Times* demonstrated how the retailer J.C. Penney had managed to game Google's system to place its site first in the list of search results for hundreds of words, ranging from "clothing" to "area rugs." Beware of these tactics and other sorts of commercial messages as you work—remember, your job is to find the best sources for your project, not those that have been paid or those that have spent the most to get noticed.

Searching with Google

Perhaps the most ambitious robot search engine, Google (*www.google.com/*) attempts to catalog the entire web by periodically visiting every known site and adding the site's text and images to its database. When you type in a keyword, it scans its database according to a predetermined set of rules and gives you a list of the results.

Google attempts to give more relevant results by ranking the listings it provides according to "popularity." Google measures popularity using a proprietary algorithm, which is based in part on how many *other* sites link to the web page in question. So, if you type `J.C. Penney SEO Scandal` in Google's search box, the first item on the list is not the *New York Times* article that broke the story, but rather a company selling its SEO services to other businesses. Google ranks this site higher in its results list, but not because the computer truly knows which site you're interested in: Google's computers can be manipulated by people who study this problem, and those in the SEO business have clearly mastered it. As a result, Google constantly changes its algorithms and uses other techniques to try to minimize the impact of these practices.

Fortunately, for most topics of academic interest, unless there is also an obvious business interest, Google searching can generate excellent results. Figure 2.2 shows the results of Jasmine's search for sites with the keywords "political polarization" and "social media." This search returned about 200,000 web pages!

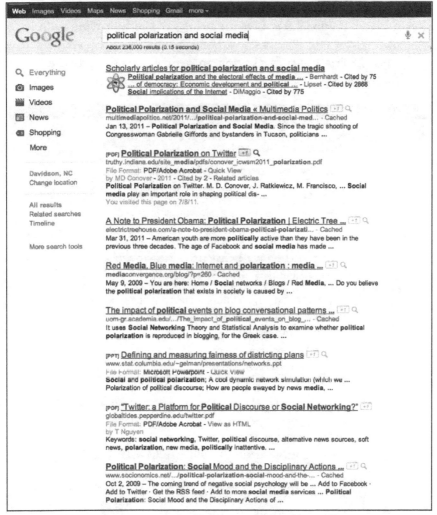

Figure 2.2: A Google search for "political polarization and social media"

Several of the top links are to journal articles and what appear to be well-reasoned opinion pieces. However, some of the links are to articles about the Twitter social network she had already found with a broader search for "political polarization and the Internet" (figure 1.2). She'd like to focus in on social media sites she hasn't already explored.

Google offers a solution: You can narrow your search by eliminating certain elements. Google will normally display only websites that include *every* search term you specify. But you can also use the minus symbol (–) to indicate search items that must not appear in the sites selected. Figure 2.3 shows the results of the following search:

```
Political Polarization and social media
-twitter
```

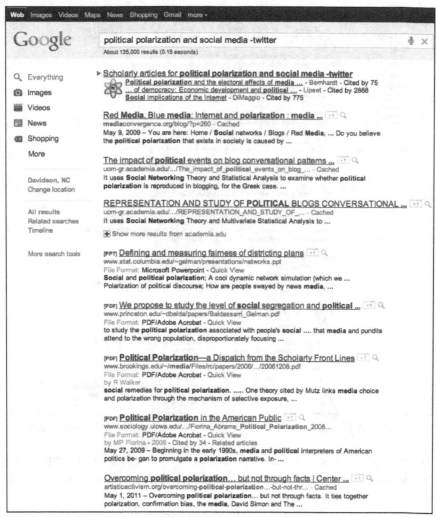

Figure 2.3: A Google search using the "minus" feature

The minus symbol specifies that the sites searched must *not* include the word (or phrase in quotes) that follows it. The search still returned about 135,000 results, including some new articles Jasmine hadn't noticed before. Although the results aren't perfect, they are closer to what she's looking for, and it's easy to scan through several pages to find what she needs.

If Jasmine is particularly interested in one aspect of social media, such as the personalized filters on Facebook that only show updates and links from friends you interact with the most, she can narrow her search further:

```
political polarization +facebook
+personalization -twitter
```

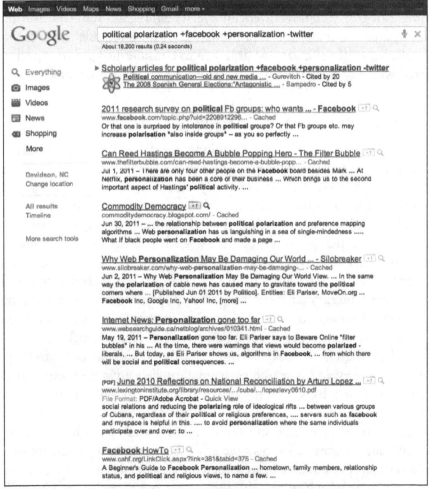

Figure 2.4: A Google search using the "plus" and "minus" features

The results this time are narrowed to 18,200 items. In some ways, this is still far too many to work with in any meaningful way. But as you can see, most of the links shown in figure 2.4 are relevant to Jasmine's interests: links to research articles she hadn't seen before, and to a blog by Eli Pariser, the author of a book on the subject, *The Filter Bubble*. A search that returns just one useful site among dozens of duds should still be considered a successful search.

Narrowing your search

The Internet can rapidly connect you to information of all kinds from around the world. Unfortunately, as the sample searches above illustrate, the web now offers an overwhelming amount of information, much of it commercial, outdated, or questionable. In order to make sense of the maze, we urge you to consider using more specialized web resources if your initial searches return lots of junk.

Advanced search strategies

Depending on what you're searching for, basic searches in search engines like Google may not be precise enough to locate the most relevant sources. This is especially true when the keywords you need to use have many different applications. For example, Jeremy Paul, a student in a "Writing about Literature" class, was particularly interested in interpretations and portrayals of Hamlet's melancholy. However, he was frustrated when his initial searches returned many references to movie versions and websites that sell low-grade literary analysis and term papers, most often used by students looking to cheat by turning in someone else's work as their own. (See chapter 5 for a discussion of plagiarism.)

Most search engines offer some form of advanced searching. Jeremy improved his search by using Google's advanced search feature (accessed by clicking the "Advanced Search" button on a Google search results page). He was then able to refine his search to locate sources providing substantial literary analysis rather than for-profit sites. Figure 2.5 shows the advanced search page—notice that Google simply builds a search for you using symbols like +, −, and quotation marks. You can also just type those directly into Google's search box once you've learned them, to obtain the same results.

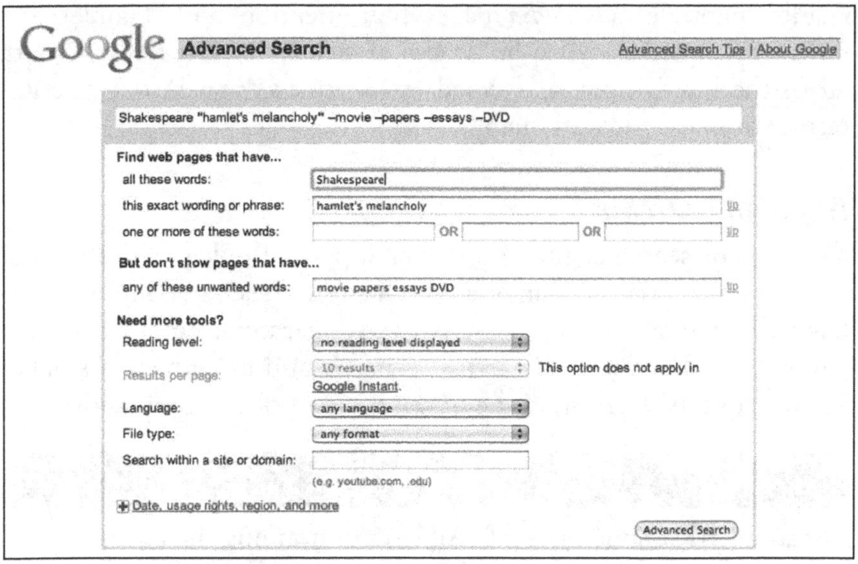

Figure 2.5: A Google advanced search

Google can also be a powerful tool for searching specific sites. For example, if you do a search on *Wikipedia* for "Hamlet," you'll be taken directly to the main *Wikipedia* page for *Hamlet.* Using Google, you can find many different pages on *Wikipedia.* Jeremy used Google's advanced search feature to refine the search. Figure 2.6 shows his

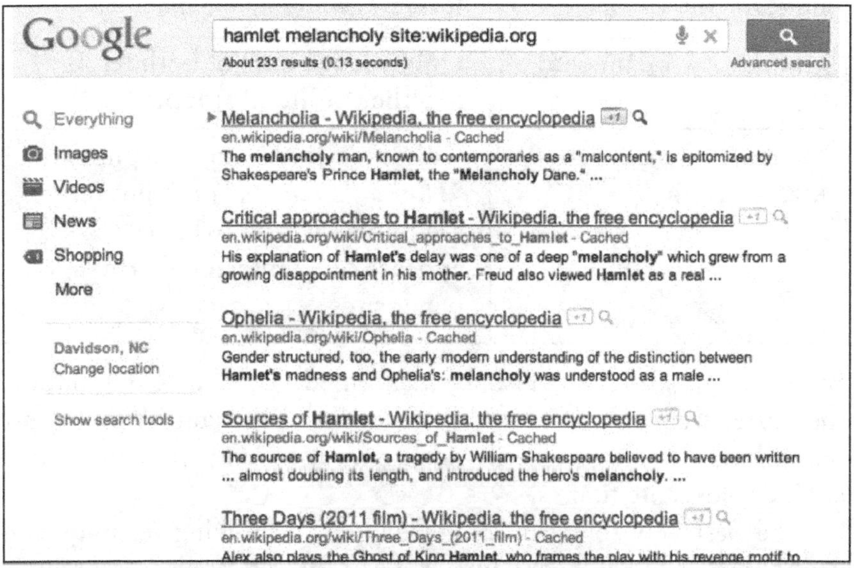

Figure 2.6: Searching for Wikipedia entries using Google

results: multiple *Wikipedia* pages that mention both Hamlet and melancholy. Jeremy typed his search terms in the "Find results with all of the words" box and typed `wikipedia.org` in the "Return results from the site or domain" box.

Boolean searching

Most major search engines no longer support **Boolean** searches, but sometimes you will encounter a search engine, such as a library database, that will allow you to use Boolean operators. Employing these commands allows you to narrow a search and bring back a smaller number of hits. Here are some of the basic Boolean commands:

Entering	Searches for
`Hamlet melancholy`	All sites containing the terms *Hamlet* and *melancholy*
`Hamlet AND melancholy`	Only sites containing both the terms *Hamlet* and *melancholy* (note that *AND* is usually necessary only when combining Boolean operators)
`Hamlet OR melancholy`	Either *Hamlet* or *melancholy*
`"Hamlet's melancholy"`	Only occurrences of both terms together (a **literal search**)
`"Hamlet's melancholy" NOT papers`	Only sites containing the phrase "*Hamlet's melancholy*" but not the phrase *papers*, which appears on commercial term paper sites

Boolean operators can also be combined. Used in combination, they offer tremendous power. For the most predictable results, use parentheses to enclose the Boolean operation you want the search engine to execute first.

The best way to learn about advanced searching techniques is probably just to try them yourself. For more on Boolean searching, check out "Boolean Searching on the Internet" at *www.internet tutorials.net/boolean.asp.*

Using the "Link" command

Another useful command available on many search engines is the "Link" command. Suppose you are interested in child psychology and have narrowed your focus to the degree of consensus or disagreement in current official statements on attention deficit hyperactivity disorder (ADHD). You have found a National Institute of Health (NIH) policy statement on the disorder and want to know every website that links to it. Simply type the following in the Google search engine, then press the "Search" button

```
Link:consensus.nih.gov/1998/1998Attention
DeficitHyperactivityDisorder110html.htm
```

Google will list any web pages in its database that contain a link back to the NIH statement. You can also use the "Link" command on Bing.

The "Link" command is a good way to find additional sources relevant to your topic, as well as sites that critique, analyze, or respond to a page you're interested in. For other specialized searches, visit the Google help page at *www.google.com/support/websearch/*.

Searching with web subject directories

While most students start research projects using a search engine, subject directories are also good places to begin a research project. People, often experts in a field, create subject directories by visiting a huge number of sites, then grouping together relevant sites with similar topics.

You can use a subject directory to help decide on a research project through a process called *tunneling*. When you visit a subject directory, you are presented with a list of general topics. You click on the topic that interests you, and a list of subtopics appears. You can continue selecting subtopics until you arrive at a list of websites on your specific topic. Then you can read each site's description and decide if it's relevant to your project.

When you've decided on a topic and are conducting in-depth research, subject directories can still be useful. You can type in a keyword and search through the subject headings to locate sites indexed by your subject directory or use tunneling to locate additional sources.

Searching with Open Directory

The Open Directory Project (*www.dmoz.org*) draws on an intriguing concept in subject directories. Tens of thousands of volunteer editors have cataloged millions of websites into a hierarchical structure. Each editor claims some expertise in a particular area

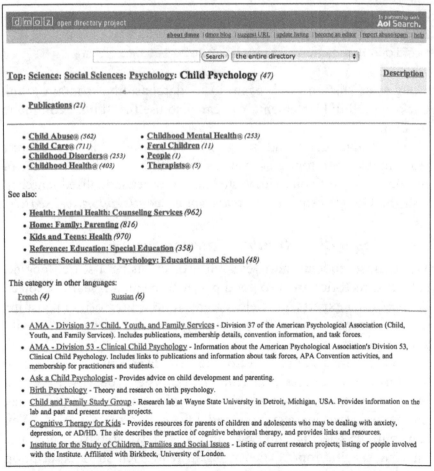

Figure 2.7: The Child Psychology page on Open Directory

and handles the classification of websites within that narrow realm. Because literally thousands of volunteers are used, the Open Directory can adapt and change at a much faster rate than other, professionally created directories. On the other hand, each topic area is only covered up to the ability of its particular editor. Since the editors are volunteers, they have other obligations, and so the quality between areas of the directory is variable.

You can use both tunneling and searching to find websites on Open Directory. For example, if you were doing a project on child psychology, you could either follow the menus supplied by Open Directory to locate sites, or you could simply type child psychology in the "Search" box on the Open Directory home page. Figure 2.7 shows the results of clicking on the child psychology subdirectory in Open Directory.

Open Directory's greatest strength—human indexers—is also its worst weakness. What an Open Directory editor deems irrelevant may be completely relevant to you. You have no way of knowing what's been left out by the human indexer. As is always the case, rely on more than one generalized search in order to ensure that you are getting all relevant information.

Another, less comprehensive index is the Internet Public Library Resources by Subject (*www.ipl.org/div/subject/*). This site lists only high-quality sites and provides reviews. Navigating the site is easy as well.

Searching for individuals

Many sites, including Yahoo! (*people.yahoo.com/*) and ZabaSearch (*zabasearch.com*) have "white pages" options that allow you to search for an individual's email or physical address. The only problem with this function is that you usually need to know more than an individual's name in order to be sure you've got the right person. Suppose you type John Smith into Yahoo!'s people search—you could end up with hundreds of listings. Take care, too—these sites often point you to fee-based "detective" services you probably don't need.

In academic research, you may be interested in finding a faculty member at a college or university. In this case, it could be easier to go directly to that institution's home page and look for a `Search` function. How do you find the institution's URL? Do a Yahoo! search.

Advanced browsing techniques

You can often speed up your browsing by taking advantage of the fact that large institutions usually have easily remembered domain names. For example, you could perform a Yahoo! search to look for Harvard University's website, or you could make an educated guess—just type `www.harvard.edu` in your browser's location box. In fact, both Firefox and Explorer will accept partial URLs—just `harvard.edu` works fine. If you're looking for a corporate site, these browsers will even guess the server name and domain type correctly. Typing just `microsoft` will bring up *http://www.microsoft.com/*.

Conducting more specialized searches

Using Google Scholar

One sophisticated resource is Google Scholar, a service of Google that emphasizes professional literature, including peer-reviewed papers, books, abstracts, and articles. A generalized Google search for ADHD returns a range of materials, including drug advertisements and sites aimed at educating the general public (see figure 2.8). In contrast, a Google Scholar search, which you conduct by selecting "Scholar" from the "More" menu on the Google toolbar (or by going to *scholar.google.com*), returns a streamlined list of sources, all from scholarly publications (figure 2.9).

Using specialized research sites

Using search engines alone won't direct you to some of the most valuable sites on the web. Although they are improving, Internet search engines often index only websites—not the information contained in databases located on the web. In addition to online magazines, most major newspapers, news magazines, and television news networks have huge, searchable websites that allow you to find an immense array of documents on news events. The major search engines might not index articles, photos, and other documents from these sites, so the only way to locate these documents is to go directly to the source.

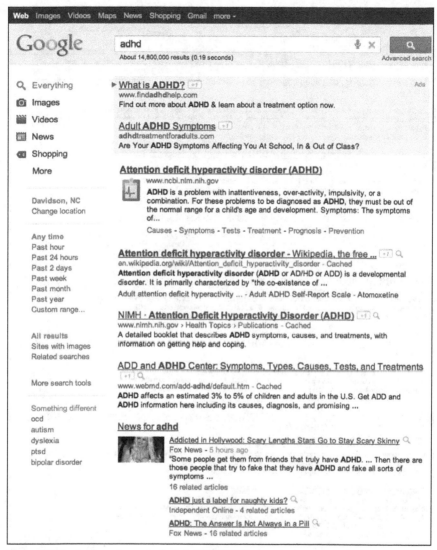

Figure 2.8: A Google search for "ADHD"

News sites

Many people now read almost all their news online by logging onto newspaper and news organization websites. If you need to find news stories on a topic more than a few days old, bear in mind that many newspapers charge a fee for searching their archives online. You might be able to get older news stories for free from a database at your library—LexisNexis Academic, for example. Check your

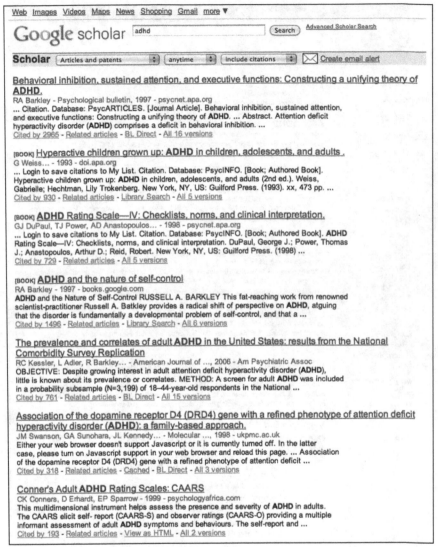

Figure 2.9: A Google Scholar search for "ADHD"

library website to see which newspaper and magazine databases it subscribes to. Here are some newspaper websites:

New York Times
nytimes.com/

Washington Post
washingtonpost.com/

Seattle Times (Offers free unlimited search of its archives.)
seattletimes.nwsource.com/

Online magazines

The web offers many online magazines or **e-zines**. These publications function exactly like printed magazines but offer their information only in an online format. Because they are distributed solely online, they can also offer features not available with traditional printed publications, such as audio recordings, interactive surveys, and continually updated message boards.

Some e-zines are available for free, but others, such as *Salon*, the oldest and most widely read e-zine, charge a subscription fee for users to access some of their more popular features. Note that most e-zines make little pretense at unbiased coverage. While *Salon* (*www.salon.com*) is seen as quite liberal; *Politico* (*politico.com*) is often seen as representing conservative opinions.

Online libraries

While the vision of the Internet as a sort of vast library containing the entire store of human knowledge has yet to be realized, several sites are beginning to take a crack at the idea. Free sites such as Project Gutenberg and Bartleby.com provide searchable texts of works that have entered the public domain. Google Book Search has the ambitious goal of searching online inside of millions of books, even many copyrighted texts; however, the site sometimes limits what you can see inside these texts to brief snippets.

Project Gutenburg
promo.net/pg/

Bartleby.com
bartleby.com

Google Book Search
books.google.com

Searching dynamic sources: Social media and blogs

The web began as a simple system for sharing information: a way for scholars to quickly and easily collaborate by placing documents in a central location where everyone could find them. But the arcane language used to format those documents—especially if the documents were going to look good—wasn't as easy as just typing up a paper in Microsoft Word. Today, however, the web offers nearly an infinite array of tools for individuals to publish information that not only looks good, but can be easily changed or commented on by others. This new web, often referred to as Web 2.0, is so powerful that despite its limitations, millions of students, scholars, and other researchers now find it to be one of the most effective ways to find and share ideas.

Searching social media

You have probably used **social media** sites like Twitter (*twitter.com*) and Facebook (*facebook.com*) to connect and share photos and links with your friends. But these sites aren't just for fun; experts in many fields also use social media to share and discuss the latest research with their colleagues. You can tap into these conversations to get up-to-date information about a wide variety of subjects.

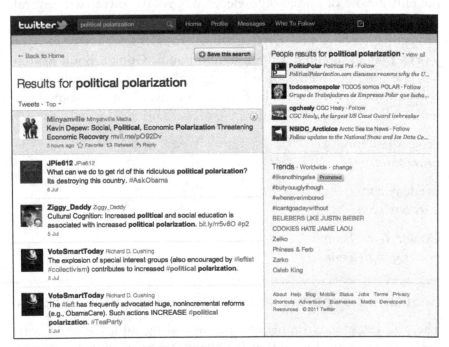

Figure 2.10: A Twitter search for "political polarization"

Jasmine typed `political polarization` in the search bar on Twitter and got a list of the most recent posts including those words (figure 2.10). While not all the posts are useful, she did find a link to a new study she hadn't seen before. She can also save this search and check it from time to time to see if other Twitter users find any other studies that might be helpful. In addition, Twitter suggests people to follow who might be relevant to the search. The first suggestion is for the Twitter account of a website, PoliticalPolarization.com. Following that Twitter account for a week or so might provide Jasmine with additional insights for her research.

Searching Facebook is not quite as useful as Twitter because Facebook's search is narrower. You can type a term in the search bar on Facebook, but the first listings will all be from your existing network of friends, which won't help when you are researching a new topic. However, if you click on "See more results" at the bottom of the search window, you will be shown some listings that might be useful. You can specify whether to search for groups, posts, people, or many other types of Facebook entries.

Searching blogs

Many conversations started on social media sites continue on blogs—or vice-versa. Twitter is great for quickly pointing people to an article or video they may not have seen, but when people want to discuss a topic at greater length, they'll often write about it in blogs.

The **blogosphere** has gotten a bit of a bad reputation in the media for being a rumor mill filled with blustering opinions and little else—and there *is* plenty of that going around there—but there's also plenty of carefully reasoned argument, expert analysis, and thoughtful reporting of real-time events. How do you find the most thoughtful blog posts? Many of the best blogs are sponsored by news organizations: The *New York Times* has blogs written by Nobel Prize winners, and magazines like *Discover* and *Scientific American* have dozens of blogs written by experts in their fields.

You can expect to find results from news blogs mixed in with the results from search engines, or from Google's news-specific search at *news.google.com*. Another good resource for finding blogs and posts by experts is Research Blogging (*researchblogging.org*), a site edited by one of this text's authors, Dave Munger. This site collects only the best posts from over 2,000 bloggers, many of them experts in their field. Bloggers are required to submit only posts supported by peer-reviewed research, and posts are organized by topic, so you can search for only the topics that interest you. Figure 2.11 shows the results of a search for "ADHD" on Research Blogging. Note that the results include not only links to the blog post discussing the research, but also to the journal articles where the research appears.

Searching with Google Blog Search

To find a wider array of blogs, try Google Blog Search (*blogsearch.google.com*). Since Google Blog Search doesn't restrict searches to blogs discussing published research, you can find many more results with it than with Research Blogging—but since no editor oversees the bloggers appearing on Google Blog Search, it's also possible that you'll get less reliable results. For example, a search for "ADHD" on Google Blog Search came up with some commercial and **spam** sites devoted to selling products rather than giving reliable information. See chapter 3 for more information on how to decide if a source is reliable.

Tracking search terms using RSS and email

One of the best reasons to use the Internet to inform your academic research is its freshness. New studies and articles are published online every day; blogs are updated even more frequently. Your research project may take many weeks to complete, so if you searched for "ADHD treatment guidelines" two weeks ago, don't assume that no new research has come out since then.

Fortunately, there is a built-in standard for staying current with online sources: syndication. The most common system for syndication is **RSS**, and most people use "RSS" to refer to any regularly updated material that is available for syndication. By subscribing to a syndicated feed, you can be alerted to these updates however you like.

To continue with the above example, you can search Web of Knowledge in your library's database for "ADHD treatment guidelines," then save that search and create an alert—either RSS or email—when a new article is published featuring those search terms. See *www.lib.berkeley.edu/BIOS/isi_alerts_2007.html* for detailed

Figure 2.11: A Research Blogging search for "ADHD"

instructions on creating the alert. How do you see the alerts? Use an RSS reader. One of the most popular is Google Reader (*reader.google.com*). You can login with your Google account and subscribe to as many feeds as you like using the "Add a Subscription" button. Then every time you visit the site, the newest items in your feed will appear at the top, whether they are blog posts, journal citations, or news articles. There are also reader apps for smartphones, dedicated computer applications, and other online sites that can handle RSS feeds.

3

EVALUATING
SOURCES

When seeking information for academic purposes, students report that they most often consult, in the following order, their course readings, search engines, scholarly databases, and their instructors. Taken together, these sources will yield a wide range of information. Course readings, such as textbooks or scholarly books or articles, represent a traditional printed source of information. Searching in a scholarly database (which we discussed in chapter 2) for information on a subject will also lead you to scholarly books, collections of essays, and articles from professional journals. Search engines, also discussed in chapter 2, will return results ranging from articles in academic disciplines to citations for scholarly books as well as blogs, newspaper articles, and sometimes images or videos.

With so much information available, you want to evaluate possible sources carefully and select the most appropriate for your project. This chapter offers tips for evaluating sources. We will explain key differences between what can be called **dynamic sources** and **static sources**, and appropriate and inappropriate uses of these resources for research. We will then discuss how to tell if sources are credible and relevant. We end with tips for keeping track of your research process in order to ensure more effective, efficient research.

Select sources based on the demands of your project

Each project has different demands. A thesis paper on Shakespeare's *Hamlet* may require that you compare the second quarto and First Folio versions. A two-page outline for an in-class presentation on the stage history of Polonius's death scene will require images from various productions, such as those available online. You want to begin by clarifying course requirements and expectation with your instructor, focusing on the following key issues:

1. **Type of source.** Often instructors discourage the use of general information sources (such as print or online encyclopedias and specialized dictionaries) in final papers, though you may consult these early in the process to get an overview or help narrow your focus. Your instructor may require that all, or a certain number, of your research sources be from academic books or refereed journal articles. For a different assignment, perhaps your instructor will require that you interview an expert. You may make that contact, and even conduct the interview, via the Internet. Check with your instructor to see what type of sources are required, expected, or discouraged, if any.

2. **Number of sources.** Whenever we have assigned research projects, at least one student will raise his hand and ask, "How many sources do we need?" This question often reflects previous experiences in secondary research, when students had to include a specified number of sources. But in college research, there usually isn't a "right" number: The number of sources needed hinges on the type of sources you are using and the type of question you're trying to answer. Along the way to narrowing down the sources you will use, you will most likely locate, scan, and consider some, but discard others—sometimes many others. In other words, instead of thinking in terms of a minimum number you need to find, finding that number, and stopping the research process at that point, consider your research as a process akin to fishing with a net. You cast the net out, pull it back in, sort through what you've found, and then discard some items while keeping others as possibly useful. Then, you cast the net out again and repeat the process as needed.

3. **Timeliness.** In some classes and for some projects, you will need to focus on recent research only. In many cases, the

Internet can provide more up-to-date information than traditional print sources. In the sciences, you may find refereed journal articles available online prior to the print release of a journal. In the humanities, you might need to seek out reviews of a current musical or art exhibition, which would be available online. But the importance of timeliness again depends on the type of course and assignment.

Always begin the research process by clarifying instructor expectations. Then, as you start digging into your sources, evaluate them carefully.

Evaluate all your sources

Instructors expect you to assess potential sources carefully, rather than take whatever you find at face value. Therefore, you want to be sure to take advantage of the print and online resources available in and through your college library, all of which have been carefully selected. Experts review scholarly books before accepting them for publication, and these books are reviewed after publication as well. Articles go through an extensive peer-reviewed evaluation of their methods and results before being accepted to scholarly journals. College librarians work with academic disciplines on their campuses to ensure that the library collects or has access to the best scholarship available though relevant indexes, databases, and interlibrary loan. Overall, the gatekeepers of academic research strive to guarantee that any source in a college library exceeds a basic standard of credibility and reliability.

In contrast to the methodical pace of academic research and publication, the Internet allows faster and more open conversation. For about ten dollars, anyone can register a web address and have as much of a web presence as Microsoft or Amazon.com. You can go to any number of host sites and create a blog where you can post your evolving thoughts and comments on issues important to you. Also for free, you can contribute to a wiki, sharing your killer shrimp quesadilla recipe with the cooking world or submitting a modification to the *Wikipedia* entry on alternative country music.

Yet, in the case of most of the above examples (*Wikipedia* being a partial exception), the Internet has no gatekeeper (for that matter, it has no single, central gate). The Internet's universality is positive because it allows previously marginalized voices to be heard, but since the Internet lacks gatekeepers, an Internet search may lead you to the ideas of an unqualified individual. Some sites seem legitimate, but an author's careless incorporation of information from other sources amounts to plagiarism. Using such a site as one of your sources—even if you did not know that some material was taken verbatim from a scholarly article without citation—only compounds the error. (We will discuss avoiding plagiarism in greater depth in chapter 5.) In short, you want to evaluate any Internet sources carefully.

Learn to distinguish dynamic sources from static sources

A decade ago, instructors might have required students to use only print sources for a research assignment, on the assumption that printed material was of higher academic quality than anything available online. Today, however, the difference between print and online sources is often unclear. Some scholarly journals you will find through accessing a library database are only available in an online format, and you will often receive actual pictures (**PDF**s) of journal articles when you order something through interlibrary loan. In this case, there may be no difference between getting the journal yourself and copying an article or ordering the digital version.

A more useful way to distinguish between types of sources is to think of them as **dynamic** (changing, often electronic) or **static** (unchanging, often print). Each type has strengths and weaknesses. Therefore, deciding when to use which type of source isn't just a matter of applying a simple formula.

To determine what type of resource will be most valuable for your project, you'll first need to consider how you are planning to use the source. Table 3.1 summarizes the most important differences between dynamic and static sources, but remember that there are many types of printed and online sources—these guidelines don't apply to all cases.

Dynamic Sources	Static Sources
Blogs, forums, wikis, newspaper sites, JPGs, websites	*Books, Journal articles, PDFs, audio files, videos*
Can include many different media.	Often only include text and images.
May appear different to different users.	Appear the same to each user.
Allow input from users.	Do not allow user input.
Inexpensive to produce.	Relatively expensive to produce.
Allow almost anyone to publish information.	Publishing closely monitored by "gatekeepers" such as editors and librarians.
Generally not subjected to scholarly review.	Often reviewed by scholars for accuracy and relevance.

Table 3.1: Comparison of dynamic and static sources

Suppose you are interested in researching ADHD in the United States. If you need authoritative information about the diagnosis of this disorder and educational accommodations required for it, books and journal articles will probably offer the most reliable information. But dynamic sources you access online will provide the most up-to-date statistics on total diagnosis in the United States today, a blog by a college student who gives first-hand accounts of her experiences, or breaking news concerning clinical trials of new drugs to treat the disorder. You might want both types of information, or only one, depending on the direction of your research.

Dynamic and static sources can offer different types of information, but they may also offer the same information. For example, you can find the text of thousands of classic works of literature, such as *Hamlet*, on the web, and you can also find many of the same works in your school library. Sometimes, you may find a source both in print form and in an online presentation. These versions may differ: Internet resources may feature graphics, sound, and video, for example. They may have a more (or less) impressive appearance than traditionally-published articles, particularly if you have an HTML copy instead of a PDF. In some cases, the online versions may be abbreviated, lacking relevant tables, graphs, and charts—or even the author's credentials. In this case, you want to assess the fuller print version of the source.

How do you decide which type of sources to use in your research? The answer depends on:

- How you'll be using the information (for what kind of project, for example).
- The degree to which the versions are identical and equally accurate.

Assess all sources for credibility

While academic books and refereed journal articles have already met a basic standard of credibility in order to be published or purchased, you want to ensure that others in the field find an argument persuasive. Check to see if the study you found has been cited by other experts. If it's been out for ten years, but no one else has referenced it in subsequent research, what are you to make of this? There are multiple ways of checking citations. If you search for attention deficit hyperactivity disorder with Google Scholar, as shown in figure 3.1, results for each source include information on how many other studies have cited it.

If you click on one of the "Cited by" tabs below a source, you are taken to the sources that cited this source. You could discover additional sources through this process, or you may realize that a source you were interested in has not been cited frequently in the literature, which in some cases might lessen its credibility.

Libraries also offer multiple databases that allow you to track citations. At present, the most robust is Web of Knowledge, which allows you to search and track citations in a host of journals published in the humanities, social sciences, and sciences. If your research requires you to explore scholarship from more than one discipline, Web of Knowledge can be useful in helping you check the credibility of your potential sources. The world of databases

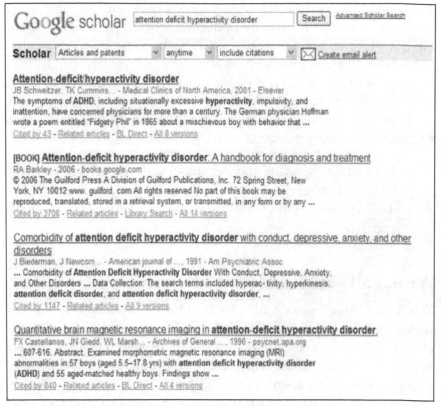

Figure 3.1: Google Scholar search showing citation counts

changes rapidly, and more are including the functionality to search citations. Check in periodically with your library to see what new tools they have for this purpose.

When you are evaluating dynamic sources, such as online discussion groups, blogs, or wikis, you need to ask lots of questions. Is the author of that forum post an expert in her field, a public figure who is paid by a political action committee, or a high school student? Does the blog you've been reading about political polarization have merit, or does it convey the rantings of a discredited reactionary? Is an article you find online based on sound scientific research, or uninformed speculation?

Because of the anonymity the Internet confers, online discussions are difficult to evaluate. It's impossible to be sure who you're conversing with, and therefore it's nearly impossible to assess the reliability of such a source. However, online discussions are a great place to get ideas for research, so you should feel free to consult them. Just be sure you can independently verify the ideas through a more reliable scholarly source.

Select sources based on relevance

Beyond credibility, you want to concentrate on relevance and filter out any irrelevant results. While authorial credentials, potential biases, publication reputation, reviews, and citations all speak to credibility, it is more difficult to offer specific advice about checking the relevance of potential sources. What makes a source relevant depends in part on what role it may play in your argument.

For example, if Jeremy is seeking to determine if Hamlet would be considered as having a specific psychological condition, such as bipolar disorder, he would need to turn to the best and latest in clinical psychology to guide his search. If, however, he was interested in exploring how portrayals of Hamlet in different film versions relate to contemporaneous conceptions of madness, he would need to look across disciplines, perhaps drawing on scholarship from history, psychology, and performance theory. In short, relevance hinges on what your topic is, what discipline you are working within, who studies that topic, and what use you intend to make of the information.

There are multiple questions you can ask about potential sources as you assess them for your projects, as shown in table 3.2 below.

Aspect	Questions
Credibility	• Who is the author? Does the author have an academic or professional affiliation? • Is a link to the author's home page and/or email provided? • Who is the sponsor of the resource? An academic organization? A business? A publication? A political action committee? • What are the potential biases of the author or sponsor? • What is the resource's purpose—to inform? To argue for a position? To solicit business or support?

Aspect	Questions
Content	• Is the resource regularly updated? • Can you verify the accuracy of the information presented? • How are sources, statistics, and images documented? • On what basis are links selected? Are all links up to date? • Are the articles reviewed by peers? • How comprehensive is this website?
Audience	• What level of audience does this seem to be written for? • Who comments on the source? How substantial are the comments? • Who links to this web page or blog?
Design	• Does the resource follow good design principles? • Are charts and graphs well labeled and clear? • Does the source contain typos and errors? • Is the website easy to navigate and use?

Table 3.2: Questions for evaluating websites, blogs, and other online resources

Let's apply these questions to two websites. Figure 3.2 shows a page from a site (*sciencebasedmedicine.com*) that answers the questions presented in table 3.2. The site is well designed, gives information about the author's credentials, and is regularly updated. Each article on the site includes the date it was created and a link to the original source it is based on. The site is free of errors, and is easy to navigate and use.

Other sites may be more difficult to evaluate. Consider the multiple blogs made available through *Discover Magazine* at **blogs.discover magazine.com**. The blogs cover many aspects of science, from biology to astrophysics. If you select a specific post to read, author credentials are provided, and individual posts provide links or references to sources. Yet because the magazine is a for-profit venture, its site

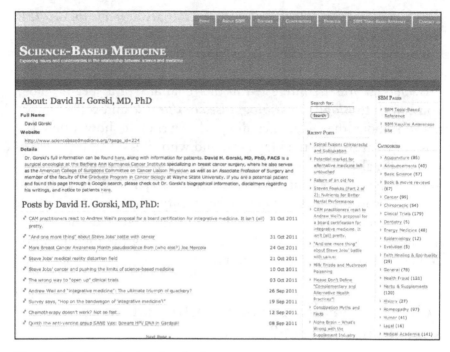

Figure 3.2: A professional web site

features advertisements. Now, does the presence of advertisements make the blogs less valid? Virtually all websites include some type of advertising as a means of funding their content. In our opinion, the mere presence of advertising does not automatically lessen a source's credibility unless the advertisers have a clear vested interest related to the site content, such as a drug manufacturer advertising next to an article about the efficacy of that drug.

Writing instructors and librarians recognize the difficulty in evaluating dynamic sources, and some have attempted to generate uniform criteria for evaluating these sources. You may want to do the Evaluating Web Pages tutorial at ***www.lib.berkeley.edu/Teaching Lib/Guides/Internet/Evaluate.html***. It offers exercises and a detailed set of guidelines on how to evaluate a website, as well as links to other sites with more suggestions.

Most guides for evaluating online sources focus on websites, but you can use many of the same strategies for evaluating other online sources, such as blogs, real-time discussions, newsgroups, or multimedia presentations. The Internet Public Library at *www.ipl.org/IPL Browse/GetSubject?vid=14&cid=1&tid=10404&cid=1&parent=0* offers a range of resources about blogs, including lists of blogs by subject, and links to blog directories, search engines, hosts, and providers. If you are interested in the reliability of a specific blog, you can go to *BlogPulse* at *blogpulse.com/profile* and collect information about the blog, including who writes it, how often it's posted, what sources the blog uses, and who cites it.

Finally, always ask yourself about any of your potential sources: What is the relative value of this resource compared to other information resources on the topic? Check with a librarian to ensure that you have explored the other resources (dynamic and static) available in this area. Never let the ease of using the Internet altogether replace a visit to your library.

What is the role of general information sources in research?

As we have discussed, students often start projects by reading a textbook, an academic encyclopedia, or *Wikipedia* to get background on a topic. Up-to-date textbooks and print or online versions of print encyclopedias (such as those offered by Gale Research) will provide you with solid academic background information available on a topic, while wikis may be updated more often and keep up with rapidly changing fields of research. Wikis are clearly a dynamic resource and can provide you with useful, current information. However, because wikis are so dynamic, they may or may not provide the most reliable or respected information on a source. For a paper on child psychology, you might browse the *Wikipedia* entry on child psychology, but then turn to a more scholarly resource, such as an encyclopedia of psychology, for further information.

Both types of sources can be quite helpful as you dig into and narrow down your possible topics, but many instructors do not consider general information sources to be valid sources for your final project. In other words, use these resources for introductory information as you explore a topic, but not as official research sources you cite in your paper.

Keep a research log as you research

The best researchers are persistent: They search, search differently, and search again if their initial queries yield too much, too little, or irrelevant information. One key to success is keeping track of where you've looked and how. Some academic librarians offer students a template to keep track of research. Even a simple strategy, such as Jeremy's partially completed log shown in table 3.3 below, can help you in this process.

Source	Search terms/limits?	Results	Comments
Google Scholar	Searched for Hamlet and melancholy.	Lots of older scholarships.	Both look promising: ordered Harvey III and printed out Flint PDF.
	Did advanced search for H and M since 2000.	Found Harvey and Flint articles.	
MLA	Searched for Hamlet and melancholy.	44 hits between 1926 and 2010.	Got PDFs of both.
		Found Gidal and Sedlmayr.	Saved citations from others in RefWorks.

Table 3.3. Sample research log

At some point in the research process, almost everybody stares at a screen, gets excited about a source, then realizes, "I looked at this already." You may go to an instructor or librarian for help in finding additional sources, only to find that person replicating searches you have already done. A log of where and how you looked and some notes on what you found can help you avoid wasting your time or anybody else's.

How do you know when you've done enough?

A research log can facilitate conversation about your research. It can also help you in making judgments about filtering out irrelevant results and knowing when you've found the best information on your topic and are ready to move on to writing. As you research, you'll readily be able to scan many sources and confidently know that some are keepers, others not worth keeping. Where students often struggle is in the middle, when confronted with a source that may or may not be useful. At this point, sometimes students freeze, unsure of what to do, or get bogged down in reading too much.

Our best advice: Go through your sources initially in a quick sort, thinking in terms of excellent, possible, and irrelevant. For the sources that might be good, spend a few minutes in a quick scan of the abstract or table of contents and make notes to yourself about the source. Then, once you hit the point in research when your new searches aren't turning up any new material, you can return to the "possible" pile and glance through it again. Does anything here add information that one of your excellent sources does not? If a source merely replicates information you have in a more recent, credible form elsewhere, then it isn't necessary.

Once you've written a rough draft and received some feedback, perhaps from the instructor or the writing center, you might decide that you in fact need more information. Maybe you have neglected to address a counter-argument, or you realize that your topic has shifted slightly. This may take you back to your "possible" pile or back into research with a specific direction in mind. Again, the better you keep track of your research in progress through a research log, the more rapidly you'll be able to find what you need to round out your argument.

Record all citation information for documentation purposes

As you research, be sure to record all information about the sources you find interesting. (See chapter 5 for how to manage this information, and chapter 6 for guidance on citation format.) Before you do so, check with your instructor to verify which documentation format to use and record all information in that format from the beginning.

4

MANAGING THE INFORMATION YOU FIND

As your research progresses, you'll begin to access a tremendous amount of material. It's temptingly easy to download everything about a particular topic. Before long, you'll end up with a collection of printouts and files that makes no more sense than the vague ideas you had when you began your project. In order for your research to be effective, you need a plan for managing the information you find.

When you start a project, you'll want to skim a few online sources to get a sense of the broad context of your chosen research topic. As you work, make a note of the sources that you think will be useful later, when you begin to learn more about your topic. You can quickly evaluate a source's usefulness by using your browser's "Find" command to look for a few key terms you know are important.

Later, as you focus and narrow your topic, you will want to go back and read these sources more carefully and follow links within them to new research materials. It's essential to set up a system that will make it easy for you to find these materials again when you need them.

Building a document management system

As you locate sources for your research, you need to be able to do two things: (1) access the information when you need it later and (2) document your sources correctly when you've completed your project (see chapter 6). In addition, any system you come up with must be able to accommodate both online and traditional sources.

Assessing the demands of your project

Not every research project is the same, so before you begin building a management system, take a moment to go over the requirements of your project. In most scientific papers, you are required to do a literature review in the introduction, summarizing previous research before reporting on your own. In other disciplines, many instructors require students to submit an annotated bibliography, which includes both a citation and a brief summary of all the sources that might be used in the final report. Many annotated bibliographies also indicate how each source contributes to the final paper's argument.

Your instructor might also require you to keep a research log, and we think it's a great idea to keep a research log as well, whether or not you have to turn it in (see chapter 3 for details). In some classes you will keep a learning portfolio, either printed or electronically, which does the same thing as an annotated bibliography, but is continually updated over the course of a semester or project. Make sure the system you use will work for all portions of your assignment, not just the research paper. That said, don't expect your software system to do everything for you. Even if your software system can't produce an annotated bibliography, you could still use it to generate a reference list, then edit that list in your word processor to generate the document you need.

Saving information about your sources

As you locate potentially useful online sources, you need to keep track of them so you can access them later if you need to. The simplest way to track web sources is to use the "Favorites" or "Bookmarks" command in your browser. However, a favorite saves only the title, URL, and access date for your source. In academic research, you need to keep all of the following information (when available) about each source you use:

- Author name
- Title (of web page, etc.)
- Title of larger work containing the source (website, etc.)
- Publication date

- URL or DOI (**Digital Object Identifier,** often used for science journal articles)
- Access date
- Brief summary of site's contents and relevance to your topic

There are lots of different options for keeping track of this information. The list below includes several.

Professional software:

- Endnote (*endnote.com*)
- RefWorks (*refworks.com*)
- Papers (*www.mekentosj.com/papers*)
- Zotero (*zotero.org*)
- Mendeley (*mendeley.com*)

Manual systems:

- Note cards (keep track of each source and quote on a 3 x 5 card).
- Word processor (type bibliographic information into a single computer file for all your sources).
- Printouts (physically print out all your sources, writing down additional bibliographic information on each source as needed). *Note:* Just having a printout is not enough! Nearly every source you cite will require you to locate additional information beyond what is available on a printout.

For small projects (with fewer than, say, twenty sources), using your word processor is probably the easiest solution. Just copy and paste the source information from your source into your word processor and type up a quick summary for later reference. To save yourself time later, format the information according to the guidelines for your discipline. See chapter 6 for guidelines on documentation using MLA and APA style.

You can use a similar method to keep track of print sources, either by copying and pasting citation data from your library's electronic catalog into a text file or by using the "Save as text" function from the electronic catalog and later transferring the text into the same file as your online sources.

Other library catalogs and online databases offer the option of emailing your citation information. If none of these options is available at your library, then print out or write down the citation data for the sources you use and type them into your computer file later. Just make sure, when you use any of these methods, that you have *all* the information you need. Three o'clock in the morning before your project is due is a bad time to realize you don't have the publication date of one of your key sources.

Using a software system to track sources

When you're working on a larger project, with dozens or even hundreds of sources, you'll need to use a more sophisticated system. It's difficult to work with a single, large Microsoft Word file, and Word's capability of searching in a group of smaller files is limited. All the professional software listed above allows you to automate this task by keeping your source information in a searchable database.

For example, you could use Zotero, a free **plug-in** that works with the Firefox web browser. To use it, you need to make sure your computer has Firefox (most computers don't come with Firefox pre-installed; you'll either be using Safari or Explorer). If you don't already have it, download Firefox from *mozilla.org* and follow the directions to install it on your computer. Then, open Firefox and use it to go to *zotero.org* and install Zotero.

Whenever you visit a web page, Zotero automatically looks for data about the sources, so if you're searching a library database or Google Scholar, or even viewing a *Wikipedia* page, it detects all the references on that page, and a manila folder icon appears in your browser's address bar. To add one or more of the sources to your list of sources, click on the manila folder, and Zotero will ask which sources you'd like to add to your library. In figure 4.1, for example, a student has searched the database at *pubmed.gov* for "ADHD treatment guidelines." He clicks the Zotero folder icon, and Zotero lists all the sources available on that page of search results, and he then selects the sources he wants to add to his library. You can organize your library into several different sub-folders, for different projects or parts of a large project.

Zotero allows you to type notes on each of your sources, and includes a link back to the source so you can find it later. When you

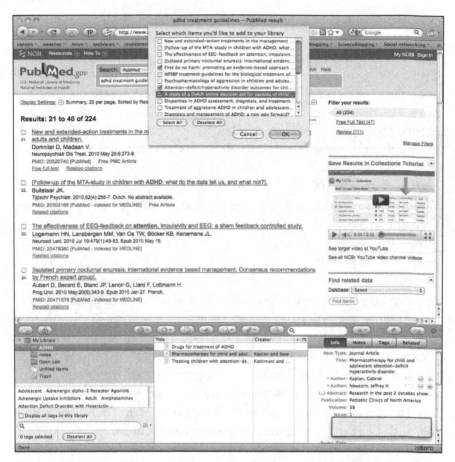

Figure 4.1: Using Zotero to keep track of information about your sources

are ready to generate your list of references or works cited, Zotero can automatically format it based on the APA or MLA guidelines we discuss in chapter 6. Endnote and RefWorks, though they aren't free like Zotero, work in a similar fashion. They also have additional advanced tools that tap directly into many schools' library databases and other professional databases.

Before you decide to invest in reference managing software, check with your librarian or instructor; your school may offer free or discounted versions of this software for students. If a particular application is recommended at your school, it probably works better within your school's library system, and it may be easier for you to get help when you need it.

Saving your source materials

Once you've saved the background information for your sources, there are two ways to save the source material itself. The first method is downloading an entire file to your computer. By choosing the "Save as" command from the "File" menu, you can save the actual text of any web page to a computer disk. With blog and forum posts, however, this can be a huge amount of information. You're probably better off just copying and pasting the text of the particular post you're interested in. Save images and other media by clicking the right-hand mouse button.

Since websites can be instantaneously changed by their creators, you'll need to preserve your source in its original form to document it for your research. It's a good idea to save the complete text of every online document you use in your research.

If your source is a PDF or other document, you can also save it to your computer so you have a permanent copy, which you can highlight or annotate using a PDF reader or an organizer like Mendeley or Papers (see "Using applications to organize your documents").

You could also print out the documents you need. Since traditional research has always relied on print sources, this might give you a sense of comfort and security as you work. But remember that whether or not a document is printed is no sure measure of reliability. Always evaluate each source you use in terms of the guidelines given in chapter 3, and remember to write down or copy and paste the information to cite the source later. Usually a printout doesn't include all the information you'll need.

Using applications to organize your documents

Keeping track of your citation data is important, but you also need an efficient way to track the vast array of PDFs and other electronic files you may collect as you do research. Mendeley (*mendeley.com*) and Papers do most of what Zotero does, but also organize the files themselves. Mendeley takes this a step further by keeping these files online, so you can access them from anywhere. If you download and install the free Mendeley application, you can work with the documents on your computer, take notes, and highlight sections of the document. Mendeley will save your changes so you can use those notes later when you're writing your report. Mendeley also syncs with Zotero, so if you have a source in one place, you can be sure it's also in the other.

Many of these systems, including Mendeley, Zotero, and Papers, go beyond merely tracking sources to become part of a social network. Students and scholars use the networks to share the papers they are reading with their friends and colleagues. You can build a research network with fellow students, and even experts in the field you're researching, to learn more about your topic. In our experience, Mendeley's network is the most widely used and potentially most useful.

TIP

Ethics: Printing and saving

When printing your sources, make sure you print only the pages you need. Some websites contain forty or more printed pages of text. Printing all of a site by mistake wastes paper and ink and costs you money. To avoid this, use the "Page setup" or "Print preview" command to make sure you're printing only the pages you need.

Etiquette

When you save files in public computer labs, make sure you put them on your own space, not the computer's hard drive (which may be periodically erased by technical staff). Some schools offer students personal server space, accessible from anywhere on the school network, and sometimes from anywhere on the Internet. Learn how to use this space, and you'll have access to your documents whenever you need them, no matter where you are. You will also avoid the possibility of losing your information due to a computer crash, as happens during crunch time at schools across the country. If such a service is unavailable on your campus, invest in a **USB thumb drive** or learn how to save files on your iPod or other device.

5

INTEGRATING SOURCES AND AVOIDING PLAGIARISM

Incorporating the voices of researchers, firsthand accounts, and experts enhances your reports and presentations by showing that your conclusions are based on solid research. Your research papers will be more effective—and get better grades—when you clearly demonstrate which ideas are your own and which come from other sources. Integrating and citing sources is so important in college that you will get into academic trouble if you don't integrate sources accurately and give them proper credit through a citation system. In addition, you can get into legal trouble if you don't get proper permission to include primary texts, such as images, video clips, and audio files that you share beyond the classroom.

In our experience, when students use material from other sources without proper attribution or citation in papers and presentations, they do so more often out of carelessness than deliberate attempts to cheat. However, from an instructor's point of view, poor integration of information from sources shows that students don't understand the purpose of research assignments. Sloppy integration hurts final grades.

And poor integration of sources can do more than hurt a final grade. Representing someone else's ideas or words as your own without proper attribution or citation is considered **plagiarism**, a theft of ideas, which can lead to failure on an assignment or in a class, academic probation, or even suspension from school. Similarly, missing or incorrect citations represent academic misconduct, whether or not the misconduct was intentional. Learning how to integrate and give credit to your sources is crucial to academic success.

In this chapter, we discuss when and how to quote, summarize, and paraphrase your sources both effectively and ethically. Academic disciplines vary in the extent to which quotation, summary, and paraphrase are used, so we give tips on how to discern the expectations within a specific subject area. This chapter also covers the legal issues surrounding the use of someone else's ideas in your work. In chapter 6, we will explain how to cite sources appropriately within the main citation systems used in academic work.

Entering the conversation

Beginning college students might think of papers as something they have to write for a grade, for an instructor who already knows the subject. They might believe the only purpose of the paper is to show their mastery of course content. While you do write papers because your instructors require them and grade them, if you only understand your papers in this way, you cheat both the writer and reader of an opportunity to learn. If you have viewed your research assignments in this light, we urge you to expand your understanding of purpose (why you write), persona (how you come across in your writing), and audience (for whom you write).

Instead, think of your papers as conversations. When you begin research, you become curious about a specific topic, develop questions about it, and pursue answers. The answers become your thesis. In the text of your paper, you enter into conversation with the sources you are using. Your audience consists of people whom you wish to persuade to consider your point, and this audience includes not just your literal reader (the instructor), but also the others interested in the ongoing conversation on your topic (in many cases, classmates, and always at least some of your sources).

Thinking of your paper as a conversation can help you avoid many of the attribution and integration errors that plague research writing. In conversation, you want to indicate which ideas come from others, which from you. You want to make clear where your ideas end, their ideas begin, and how the two relate. How would you feel if you'd told a classmate over lunch about a theory you had about a course reading, then in class that afternoon, the classmate raised her hand and presented your theory as if it is her own? She may have said exactly what you said, or she may have rephrased it slightly. In either case, you'd be aggravated, and the classmate would have lost credibility with you.

This type of inappropriate use of sources can happen in academic writing in multiple ways. Let's consider the case of Jeremy, who is interested in *Hamlet* and shifting conceptions of mental illness in the five hundred years since the play was first performed. Through Google Scholar, he found an article by a British doctor, A. B. Shaw, who argued that Hamlet doesn't seek revenge for his father's death right away because he is depressed.

Based on the abstract, Jeremy likes this article. In the following excerpt from the abstract, Shaw explains that critics have offered multiple explanations for why Hamlet delays avenging his father's death, but

> none is convincing. The interpretation that fits the evidence best is that Hamlet was suffering from an acute depressive illness, with some obsessional features. He could not make a firm resolve to act. In Shakespeare's time there was no concept of acute depressive illness, though melancholy was well known.

Because Jeremy's library doesn't have the *British Medical Journal*, he orders the article through interlibrary loan. Unfortunately, he got started on research late, and an electronic copy of the full article does not arrive before the paper is due. But even the abstract, he thinks, gives him good information, and he draws on the abstract as well as a definition of *melancholy* from an academic encyclopedia in the introduction to his paper:

> While we understand the behavior of fictional characters in relation to how our culture understands the human mind, we also need to realize that how people view human psychology has changed over time. Such is certainly the case with William Shakespeare's famous play *Hamlet, Prince of Denmark*. Today, we think that Hamlet was suffering from an acute depressive illness. Yet in Shakespeare's time, people watching the play would have thought Hamlet was sick with melancholy, which **one scholar explains** "meant much more than just sadness or

depression; it was a physical condition that could include digestive disorders and flatulence, but it regularly led to illusions, delusions, the inability to test reality, and to insanity" (Midelfort). Hamlet's melancholy would have been seen as a character defect then, as **one British doctor notes**, not an illness he needed but did not have adequate treatment for (Shaw).

Jeremy goes on to compare how an Elizabethan audience and a contemporary audience would perhaps respond differently to certain lines, based on their conceptions of psychology.

When you glance at this introduction, you will notice the attributions to sources, in boldface above, as well as the MLA parenthetical citations to Midelfort, the author of the encyclopedia article, and to Shaw. Jeremy cites both the Shaw article and the Midlefort entry on his Works Cited page. Surely there is no problem with the way Jeremy has integrated or given credit to his sources.

But there are problems. Where did Jeremy get the rather technical phrase, "Hamlet was suffering from acute depressive illness"? He got it from Shaw. But he does not quote that distinctive phrase or indicate that this was Shaw's idea. He presents the idea without any attribution in the same way that the hypothetical classmate stole your idea. Let's assume Jeremy did not intend to present Shaw's idea and words as his own, but he did. He plagiarized.

Even if he had quoted that phrase and cited Shaw in the sentence, there is another subtle problem: Jeremy cites the Shaw article on his MLA Works Cited page, but he does not use the article, only the abstract to an article that he never read. In this instance, he does not cite the correct source, giving his instructor the impression that he used a full article when he did not. This is incorrect attribution and poor academic practice that undermines Jeremy's credibility.

It isn't hard to avoid the errors that Jeremy made. With a little care and attention to detail, you can master the skills you need to integrate your sources effectively for all your classes.

Integrating your sources: three strategies

One of the challenges of the first year of college is learning to navigate the differing vocabularies and expectations you encounter in your classes. These variations reflect differences between academic disciplines, and show up in expectations for written work. In addition to mastering any specialized vocabulary you need for a field of study and using the type of sources appropriate to the field in your research, you will need to learn what strategies for integrating and citing sources are appropriate. The sections that follow cover three major ways writers commonly make use of the work of others. Though some disciplines use one strategy more than another, you will incorporate your sources effectively whatever the course assignment if you master all three.

When and how to quote

You want to quote from your sources when the exact words are important, when the point is so well said—or poorly said—that you want to emphasize the wording, or when the person saying them is an important figure. You'd quote a poem if you were conducting literary analysis. You'd quote from an ad if you were arguing how it tapped into contemporary public values. You'd quote your school mission statement if you were arguing that a curricular change would better fulfill that mission.

In order to integrate a quote effectively, you should lead into the quote, or immediately follow it, with a phrase attributing the quotation to its source. Signal phrases like "According to one expert," "Helene Intraub notes," and "Kwame Anthony Appiah describes this phenomenon as" tell the reader that you are about to bring another voice into the conversation. Good attribution also indicates the authority of the source. Perhaps you are working on a medical topic, and you have a quote from the head of the Centers for Disease Control. Indicating that person's position as well as name in the attribution only strengthens your argument.

How you give credit to the quotation in your text varies by documentation system, as we discuss in chapter 6. Yet in each of the major systems, you must indicate your debt to the text. This is also true of any images, tables, graphs, or other visual aids that you take in whole or part from other sources. The source must be cited. (We discuss this in more detail later in the chapter.)

Beyond giving effective attribution and correct citation to quotations, you have other important decisions to make. First among these is how much to quote—a few key phrases or a block of text? Students tend to over-quote instead of pruning a quote for the bit they need or using ellipses to cut out irrelevant phrases. You also may need to modify a quote. Sometimes vague pronouns need to be clarified or verb tenses changed to go with the flow of a paragraph, which can be accomplished through using brackets to indicate changes.

Even if you modify a quote to fit, make sure that you do not misrepresent what a source argues. Imagine how you would feel if you'd read an ad for a movie that included a quoted phrase from a review, "Never have I been so glad." You plan to see the movie until you track down the actual review, which in fact states, "Never have I been so glad to leave a cinema." In this example, the movie advertisers haven't plagiarized, but they have behaved unethically. Be sure in your academic work that you do not do the same by warping what somebody says.

In addition to ethical issues, you want to avoid sloppy integration of quotations. Sometimes students commit the "plop and run." By this, we mean the practice of introducing the quote by saying where it comes from, giving the quote, and then just moving on to your next point. When asked, students say that they commit plop and run because they assume the reader knows how the quote proves a point. Yet instructors and other readers do not necessarily know unless the writer explains the connections.

Perhaps the most common cause of plagiarism related to quotations stems from the ease with which we can cut and paste. A student who is not taking careful notes may find a great paragraph from an online source that she wants to use in her paper. She cuts and pastes the paragraph directly into her draft, intending to go back later and either reduce the quote to a manageable size or summarize its main point. But, in the rush of finishing a paper, she forgets to do either, perhaps also forgetting to put quotation marks around the information, or only hastily rephrasing the paragraph so that it is still mostly in the source's language. An instructor reading this paper will notice the shift in diction (word choice) and tone and recognize that a different voice, unacknowledged or incorrectly represented, has entered the conversation. To avoid this situation, we strongly recommend that you develop a thorough note-taking practice, as described in chapter 4, and that you *never* cut and paste directly from online sources into the draft of your paper.

When and how to summarize

You should quote when you need the exact words or want to borrow the authority of the person who said them. In contrast, summary is the most appropriate strategy when you need the overall point of one or even several arguments covered concisely. Summary occurs frequently in scientific articles, such as in the literature review section of articles in which authors show how previous research on a topic relates to their own research. Summary is also used, however, in the humanities and social sciences when the overall point, not the fine details, of other research is needed to provide context for your scholarly conversation.

For example, consider a sentence such as "**Previous studies have shown** a correlational link between stress and excessive mid-body fat accumulation (Jones et al. 91, Smith 92, Fredrichson 99)." This one sentence indicates that the author is familiar with previous research and is summarizing all three of these studies. While summary offers only a main point view of research, as compared to the close view offered by quotation, notice that the author still uses a signal phrase (in boldface) and gives discipline-specific citation to the studies that precede his at the end of the sentence as well as in the references section. Summarizing well means capturing the overall point of the information you want to include accurately. If you are summarizing one chapter from a book, for example, you would not want to imply that you are summarizing the whole book in your attribution. Rather, use the signal phrase to indicate what you are summarizing.

When and how to paraphrase

The third primary means by which writers integrate material from other sources into their own work is through **paraphrase**, in which the ideas of passages are represented in the writer's language. When you paraphrase, the reader should not notice a different voice entering the conversation (as happens in quotation). Rather, the reader is following your line of argument, with information from other sources smoothly integrated into that argument. Paraphrase is the best strategy for integration when the details of what is said, but not exactly how it is said, matters.

Let's say that Jasmine, the student interested in political polarization, winds up writing about how social media arguably intensify political polarization. In her paper, she wants to consider counterevidence as well and has focused in on a particular passage from an interesting article on the topic from a peer-reviewed online journal. Here is the original passage from a November 2009 article, "Getting political on social network sites: Exploring online political discourse on Facebook," by Matthew Kushin and Kelin Kitchener:

> Because Facebook is an online space where political expression occurs on profiles through friend associations with candidates and associations with groups and political applications (Williams and Gulati, 2007), there is great potential for users to receive political information about friends in their network, such as their political stances and affiliations as well as membership in political Facebook groups.
>
> These unique push features of Facebook may lead to increased inadvertent exposure to dissimilar viewpoints and ultimately lead disagreeing parties to interact in a common discussion space.

In her draft, Jasmine paraphrases Kushin and Kitchener's information in the following paragraph:

> Considerable evidence suggests that people may interface mostly with others who have the same political beliefs when they are online. The sometimes anonymous nature of the Internet in fact may encourage people to be ruder to those with whom they disagree politically. Yet other experts disagree. In their recent article, Matthew Kushin and Kelin Kitchener note that Facebook users **have the potential to receive lots of political information about their friends, including political positions and affiliations.** Thus, users might get exposed to views they don't have and perhaps lead them into discussion about topics.

Jasmine covers the information from her source fairly and uses a signal phase to indicate when she begins using their ideas, but her paraphrase comes a bit too close to the original language at the points in boldface above. She would be better off changing distinctive words from the original, such as "potential" and "affiliations," in order to ensure that she represents the source fairly but does not borrow its language without acknowledging that borrowing through quotation.

Our best advice is to ask for help when you are unsure. Ask your instructor for model papers from the course or in the subject and study how the research you're working on incorporates its sources. You might ask your instructor to look at a sample paragraph and a source paragraph to see if you are using the source appropriately. The writing center or other writing support service on your campus is another good place to go for guidance here. Above all, always ask for help in advance, not the night before a paper is due. Finally, never write rough drafts without including attribution to your sources from the beginning of the process.

Here is a brief table to help you remember the most important dos and don'ts when you are working to give credit to and incorporate your sources effectively.

Strategy	Do	Avoid
Quotation	• Lead or follow with a signal phrase indicating who you are quoting and why. • Use just what you need, no more. • Modify quotation as needed through ellipsis and brackets.	• Over-quoting, especially in fields such as science where quotes are rarely used. • Altering the meaning of the original. • Plopping a quote in without discussing how it supports your point.

Strategy	Do	Avoid
Summary	• Use a signal phrase to indicate source as appropriate: Always indicate debt to source in citation format used in class. • Accurately summarize the original.	• Misrepresenting the original. • Using somebody else's summary (e.g., an abstract) instead of your own summary.
Paraphrase	• Lead or follow with a signal phrase indicating who you are paraphrasing and why. • Be careful to transform the content into your own language and avoid lifting core phrases from the original.	• Presenting as paraphrase what is really quotation.

Table 5.1. Guidelines for using quotation, summary, and paraphrase

Understand the legal requirements of using online text and images

Here are some situations where copyright issues affect your research and writing online:

1. You download a photograph from a commercial, subscription-based web exhibition and include it in your art history paper, citing it according to MLA guidelines.
2. You want to post your essay on Gwendolyn Brooks's poem "We Real Cool" on the class blog. In your essay, you quote the entire poem—eight lines, which you typed in by hand

from your textbook—taking care to credit the author of the poem.

3. You post the entire text of the *Wikipedia* article on abortion into the comments section of a pro-life blog. You don't cite the source, since you heard that *Wikipedia* is copyright free.

4. You have collected MP3s of your twenty favorite songs and want to post them to your personal web page, housed on the campus server. Some of them come from your CDs, while you found others available online.

5. You publish a scathing critique of Jonathan Franzen's latest novel in both the print and online versions of your school newspaper, quoting the entire first paragraph and discussing its failings in detail, pointing to specific examples throughout the book and revealing a plot twist. You obtain no permission from the author or the publisher of the book.

When you reproduce a copyrighted work without the permission of the copyright holder, in most cases, you are violating the law. There are two important exceptions to the law, illustrated in examples 1 and 5 above.

Make single copies of copyrighted work for educational use

You may reproduce a copyrighted work for your personal educational use, as in a paper submitted only to your instructor or discussed in class. This is the "educational use" provision of the law.

Make many copies of copyrighted work or publish on the web if it meets fair use guidelines

You may also publish extracts from a copyrighted work if you're publishing a critical analysis or review of the work. You may not reproduce the entire work, however, and you must give credit to the original source. While applications of the law vary, as a rule of thumb, never quote more than 300 words or 10 percent of a work, whichever is less. The logic behind this rule is that copyright law protects the copyright holder's right to control sales or distribution of the work. If your use of the work enables people to obtain it from you rather than from the copyright holder, then you are violating copyright law. This is true even if you do not profit from your actions. The positive side of copyright is that as long as your comments are not libelous, the law protects your right to print even extremely negative criticism of copyrighted works without permission. This is the "fair use" provision of the law, designed to balance the right of free speech with the right of creative people to profit from their work.

Find out if a work is copyrighted before you reproduce it

Never assume a work is not copyrighted, even if you see no copyright notice. Copyright law does not require a notice—copyright laws protect any original work you produce unless you explicitly give permission to reproduce it. Here are three cases when it is acceptable to reproduce a work that is not your own without obtaining permission (but you must still give credit to your source):

1. The copyright has expired. In the United States, the law is constantly evolving, but you can be fairly certain a work's copyright has expired if the work was published before 1923. In Great Britain and much of the rest of the world, copyrights generally expire seventy years after the death of the author.
2. The author has placed the work in the public domain. Please note that except in the case of government documents, this rarely occurs.
3. The author has licensed the work as open source or open content, allowing limited use of the work without obtaining permission.

Determining whether the copyright has expired may take some research. Make sure you have determined the most recent revision date of the work you're using. For example, William Strunk's *The Elements of Style* was first published in 1909; its copyright has expired and you are free to reproduce that version of the text. However, E. B. White's revision of the text remains copyrighted; you cannot reproduce that work without permission.

Many government documents, such as the *Congressional Record*, are in the public domain. Be careful, however—even the *Congressional Record* may contain copyrighted material quoted from other sources. When in doubt, request permission.

Request permission to reproduce copyrighted work

If you make a document available to the public, you must get permission to reproduce any copyrighted material it contains. Refer to table 5.2 to determine whether you need to request permission to reproduce copyrighted material in your document.

Locating the copyright holder

To obtain permission to reproduce the work, you must first determine who holds the copyright. If you're quoting from a source on the web, look for a copyright statement, usually found at the bottom of the web page. Often an email link will be provided, and you can email the copyright holder directly. Otherwise, you may need to email the webmaster for the site to find a contact.

If the work you want to reproduce comes from a book, the copyright statement is generally found on the page following the book's title page. The copyright holder is generally the author or the publisher, but it might be someone else entirely. Make sure the portion of the book you want to reproduce has not been reprinted from some other work. If it has been reprinted, you'll probably need to locate the original source to find all the information you need. Even if the author holds the copyright for the work, the best course of action is usually to contact the publisher. Try visiting the publisher's website and searching for "permissions department." Many publishers now provide electronic links for requesting permissions. For other publications, such as newspapers and magazines, follow a similar procedure.

Use this table to determine when it is acceptable to reproduce a copyrighted work without requesting permission from the copyright holder. In each case, you must give credit to the creator. These guidelines also apply to open source/open content work, but you should refer to the license to see if it grants additional rights.

	Critical Analysis/ Review	Summary or Paraphrase	Complete or Partial Works
Text			
Paper turned in to instructor	A	A	A
Paper posted to class discussion site	A	A	E
Posting to national forum	300/10	E	N
Blog post	300/10	E	N
Website	300/10	E	N
Other Media (Images, Audio, Video)			
Paper turned in to instructor	A	A	A
Paper posted to class discussion site	A	A	E
Posting to national forum	N	E	N
Blog post	N	E	N
Website	N	E	N

A: Always acceptable
E: Educational materials only
N: Never acceptable
300/10: Acceptable to reproduce 300 words or 10 percent, whichever is less

Table 5.2. Copyright guidelines for primary material found online

Sending the letter of request

To request permission to reproduce a work, send a polite letter or email explaining how and where you wish to use the work. Explaining that you are a student and that you intend to use the work only for educational purposes will go a long way. Often this process takes several weeks and may result in permissions fees, so you probably want to have a backup plan in case you do not receive permission to reproduce the work you want.

After you receive permission to reproduce a copyrighted work, it is essential that you give the rightsholders credit as they specify; otherwise you may still be in violation of copyright law. In addition, you must give proper academic credit to your sources as specified in chapter 6.

Using open source and open content

Does tracking down rightsholders seem like an arduous task? A growing number of blogs, photos, software programs, and even videos and music on the web are now being offered under open source and open content licenses. This means the authors have agreed to let others use their materials for free, subject to restrictions they specify. While a variety of these licenses exist, the most popular are Creative Commons licenses. Creative Commons was founded by activists who were frustrated with the growing restrictiveness of copyright law. They realized that if a large amount of freely usable material was available, then others could build on those works without spending hours tracking down rightsholders.

Wikipedia is built on a similar foundation, the GNU Free Documentation License (GFDL). The GFDL is an example of a viral or copyleft license, because it requires that all publications using GFDL material are also licensed with the GFDL, thus spreading the work to a wider and wider array of users.

Other licenses restrict you to noncommercial use, or require you to give credit to the original source (something you're required to do for classwork, anyway). Generally, when you're using open source materials for classwork, properly citing the source is all you need to do (see chapter 6). Check *creativecommons.org* for more information. The Creative Commons website can also help you perform Google and Yahoo! searches for open source works that are free to use for a variety of purposes.

6

DOCUMENTING ONLINE SOURCES

As we mentioned in chapter 5, anytime you use someone else's words, images, sounds, or ideas in your academic work, you must give them proper academic credit. Although avoiding a plagiarism charge motivates us powerfully to document, the most important reason to document your sources is to help others learn from your work. Even if your paper is read only by your instructor, you may have found an idea that your instructor wants to follow up on—the result of your instructor's efforts could be a published book, journal article, or website with credit given both to you and to the sources you cite in your paper. If you publish your work on the web, you could be helping thousands of others learn from your research, and by directing them to the sources for your work, you can help them learn even more. Documenting sources consists of three steps:

1. Collecting information about your source.
2. Formatting the documentation according to your system's guidelines.
3. Integrating the source material into your project and citing it appropriately in the text.

Documentation is easiest if you collect the required information when you locate your source. A common error is to scribble down information without documentation guidelines nearby, then discover later that you omitted to collect a necessary bit of information. Later on, it may be difficult or even impossible to get that information, so always work with your documentation guidelines on hand.

If you follow a good record-keeping practice, perhaps using a reference management software that can save all your sources in a selected citation format, you should have all the information you need. Your library may offer a program like RefWorks, and you can also find inexpensive options as well as free or open source programs for this purpose. In chapter 4, we discussed two such free applications, Zotero and Mendeley. Even if you do use source management software, be sure to purchase the required handbook or citation guide and have it on hand throughout the research process, as ultimately you are accountable for the accuracy of your citations.

Determine how sources are documented for your type of project

Because research and learning take many different forms, each academic discipline has its own rules for how to document sources. For example, scholars in the humanities are most often interested in specific written words, so the author and page number (for print sources) are given in Modern Language Association (MLA) citations. In contrast, social scientists value how recently a study was conducted, so the author and date are given in American Psychological Association (APA) citations. Please note that disciplines also develop specific guidelines to cover types of documents used mostly within their research but not elsewhere, and your instructor may specify additional rules based on the needs of your class. Be sure to check on your course syllabus and with your instructor to determine the proper method of documentation in each class.

This brief guide cannot give examples for documenting every type of source in every discipline. Instead, we discuss how to document most electronic sources in the two most widely used documentation systems, MLA and APA. For more information about these styles, you can visit the relevant websites at:

www.mla.org/www_mla_org/style
www.apastyle.org/elecgeneralf.html

The MLA does not provide models for citation on its website and instead refers students to one of the organization's style manuals. This is good advice, though many websites do provide tips you can draw on in the short-term. The APA website does give basic guidelines for citing electronic sources, available at the link given above. In the remainder of this chapter, we will demonstrate how to document online sources using MLA and APA formats, covering the three steps described for each of the citation systems in turn.

Using the MLA style to document electronic sources

Collecting information about your source

Depending on what type of electronic source you are working with, MLA documentation will require some of the following elements:

- The author's name or its equivalent—such as a login name or alias. Sources may also have multiple authors, an organizational or group author, or no known author. If there is no author, but the source has an editor, you list that name, followed by **Ed.** (If you have both an author and an editor, the editor's name comes later in the entry, as in example 5 below.)
- The title of a long work—such as a book, play, or entire website—in italics; shorter sources, such as a poem, short story, article, website section, blog, email, or other online posting in quotation marks.
- If your electronic source appeared originally in print, you next include full publication information for the print version (consult the most recent version of the *MLA Handbook* for citation details, which are also contained in many writing handbooks).
- If you are using a portion of a website which you have already cited, you then need the title of the website (personal or professional) in italics; if a website has no title, describe it as accurately as possible (e.g., **home page**).

- Other identifying information about the electronic source (such as volume or issue number for an online journal) or version number for a project, if any.
- The name of the publishing or sponsoring organization, followed by a comma. If you cannot find a publisher, use **n.p.** ("no publisher") instead.
- The date the site was created or updated (if available) *or* the date the post or email was made. If you cannot find a date, use **n.d.** ("no date") instead.
- The medium of publication (**web**).
- The most recent date you accessed the site in date/month/year order.

In its most recent edition, the MLA no longer requires that you include the URL of online sources. If you think that a reader would not be able to readily find a source online without that information, then you should put the URL after your date of access, inside angle brackets, with a period after the closing bracket. Examples 1, 9, and 10 below illustrate the inclusion of an URL.

As mentioned previously, not all sources will have all of these elements. Figure out what type of source you have by looking through the models listed below and then collect all necessary information. If you are not sure you have the right model, pick the one closest to your source and make time to clarify proper citation format with your instructor.

Formatting your citations

List all the sources you use on a separate page (or pages), titled **Works Cited**. Arrange the entries alphabetically, by author's last name or by title if no author is given, and double-space the entire page, both within and between entries. The first line of each citation is flush left, and all subsequent lines of a citation are indented five spaces.

For a detailed discussion of all citation models, please refer to the most recent edition of the *MLA Handbook* or to a handbook that draws on the most recent edition. We cover here models for most common electronic sources.

1. Website (home page)
Website with institutional or corporate sponsor

> *Folger Shakespeare Library: Advancing Knowledge and the Arts*. Folger Shakespeare Library, 4 March 2005. Web. 17 July 2011.

Personal website

> Munger, Dave. *Science-Based Running*. N.p., June 2011. Web. 19 July 2011.

Government website

> United States Department of Health and Human Services. "Attention Deficit Hyperactivity Disorder (ADHD)." *The National Institute of Mental Health*. Updated 5 July 2011. Web. 20 July 2011. <http://www.nimh.nih.gov/health/topics/attention -deficit-hyperactivity-disorder-adhd/index.shtml>.

2. Book

> Wordsworth, William, and Samuel Taylor Coleridge. *Lyrical Ballads, with a Few Other Poems*. London: Arch Publishers, 1798. *Project Gutenberg*. Project Gutenberg Association, January 2006. Web. 18 July 2011.

3. Poem or short story

> Brooks, Gwendolyn. "We Real Cool." *The Bean Eaters*. 1960. *Poets.org*. The Academy of American Poets, 2011. Web. 21 July 2011.

Poe, Edgar Allan. "The Cask of Amontillado." 1846.

Poe Museum. N.p., 2010. Web. 21 July 2011.

4. Book review

Review of *Babies by Design: The Ethics of Genetic Choice* by Ronald M. Green. *Bioethics.com*. N.p., 20 January 2009. Web. 21 July 2011.

5. Encyclopedia article

Wilson, George. "Action." *Stanford Encyclopedia of Philosophy*. Ed. Edward N. Zalta. Stanford University, 29 August 2009. Web. 21 July 2011.

6. Journal article
First published in print

Fuggetta, Giorgio, Silvia Lanfranchi, and Gianluca Campana. "Attention Has Memory: Priming for the Size of the Attentional Focus." *Spatial Vision* 22.2 (2009): 147–159. *Ingentaconnect*, 2009. Web. 20 July 2011.

Internet publication only

Kushin, Matthew J. and Kelin Kitchener. "Getting Political on Social Network Sites: Exploring Online Political Discourse on Facebook." *First Monday* 14.11. 2 November 2009. N.pag. Web. 14 July 2011.

7. Magazine article

Davidson, Adam. "The Emerging Epicenters of High Tech Industry." *Wired*. June 2011. Web. 21 July 2011.

8. Newspaper article

Article from print edition accessed online

> Vartabedian, Ralph and W.J. Hennigan. "NASA's Heady
>
> Goals Darkened by Clouds." *Charlotte Observer*.
>
> 21 July 2011: A1. Web. 21 July 2011.

Article from online newspaper

> Rogers, Christina Ritchie. "Towns Want More Say on
>
> Visit Lake Norman Board." *Davidsonnews.net*. 19
>
> July 2011. Web. 22 July 2011.

9. Image, audio, or video file

> Vermeer van Delft, Johannes. *The Guitar Player* 1672.
>
> *WebMuseum, Paris*. 14 October 2002. Web. 22 July
>
> 2001. <http://www.ibiblio.org/wm/paint/auth
>
> /vermeer/>.

10. Posting

Blog

> Badger, Emily. "Political Polarization Grows as Job
>
> Security Falls." *Miller-McCune.com*. N.p., 19
>
> July 2011. Web. 21 July 2011.

Forum

> Kaku, Dr. K. T. "Buddhist Psychology and Cognitive
>
> Behavior Therapy: Strange Bed Fellows?" *Behavior*
>
> *Online*. N.p., 25 March 2005. Web. 21 July 2011.
>
> <http://www.behavior.net/bolforums/showthread
>
> .php?t=411>.

11. Personal email message

```
Kelpin, Peter. "Re: Edits." Email to the author. 20

    July 2011.
```

Integrating source materials

When you begin creating your project, whether it is a research paper, oral presentation, poster, or website, you need to credit your sources each time you quote, summarize, or paraphrase information from them. In MLA, credit is indicated with a parenthetical citation (also called an in-text citation). For print sources, this normally includes the author's last name and the page cited: `(Nelson 29)`. If you are working with an article in a PDF, you can cite page numbers because this universal file format retains the fonts, images, graphics, and layout of the original document.

In other cases, when a source includes fixed numbering (such as numbering of paragraphs), then cite the relevant numbers. Give the appropriate abbreviation before the numbers: `(Jones pars. 4-6)`. (*Pars.* is the abbreviation for *paragraphs* as listed in the *MLA Handbook*).

Because electronic sources often lack page numbers, these entries do not require parenthetical citation in the text. But, you want to make sure that your reader can locate your source on the Works Cited page, so we recommend that you include in your signal phrase (discussed in chapter 5) the first item from the works cited entry, which would be the author's name in most cases, and at least a short version of the title of the piece in all other cases. Here's an example of a signal phrase that would tell a reader what source the information comes from:

> **In her online article,** Amanda Mabillard explores the function of "sullied" in Hamlet's soliloquy from Act One, Scene Two.

If curious about Mabillard's argument, the reader can then refer to the Works Cited page for more information about the reference.

If you have more than one work by an author in your research, also include an abbreviated version of the title in parentheses to distinguish which source you are using: `(Campbell "help")`. Try to make your references to sources as inconspicuous as possible. Your goal is to give the reader enough information to locate the source on your Works Cited page, not to interrupt the flow of your argument.

Using the APA style to document electronic sources

While MLA is used widely in the humanities, APA is used frequently in the social sciences and sciences. Be sure you check with your instructor, however, to find out which documentation system your class is required to use.

Collecting information about your source

As the American Psychological Association notes, electronic sources vary wildly. Online articles follow the same guidelines as for printed articles. Depending on what type of electronic source you are working with, APA documentation requires at least these elements:

- The author's name or its equivalent when the actual name isn't provided, followed by the date of publication, in parentheses. (If there is no author, the title leads the reference and is followed by the date.)
- The title of the document within the scholarly project, database, or periodical; *or* the title of the discussion list posting or blog in plain text (i.e., not in quotation marks or underlined).
- The title of the website (personal or professional), scholarly project, database, or periodical in italics. If the publication is a periodical, end this information with a comma. If anything else, end with a period.
- If you are working with an article from a periodical, next give the volume and issue number, as in the following example: 4 (2). If you have a PDF of the original article, also include page numbers.
- If you are using an entry from a blog, a podcast, or a graph, indicate the medium in brackets, as in example 8 below.
- If the work has a **Digital Object Identifier** (DOI), include that number after the title, preceded by **Retrieved from**. If you do not have a DOI, end with the URL, again preceded by **Retrieved from**. If you think the source is updated frequently, include

the date of retrieval in that phrase (e.g., "Retrieved on 18 July 2011 from").

You can simplify your challenge if you work to guide your readers directly to the source of the information you include in your paper. However, online materials sometimes change URLs. So, the most recent APA edition recommends that references include a Digital Object Identifier instead when available. DOIs are linked to individual documents and consist of a long alphanumeric code. A database ensures that the document is always available, even if its URL changes. At present, many publishers will provide an article's DOI on the first page of the document.

If you cannot find a DOI, that does not mean the document doesn't have one; the DOI may be available when you click a button labeled "Article" or on an abbreviation of the name of the service that is making the article available, such as Wiley Online Library. If you are having difficulty finding a DOI for an APA-style paper, ask your reference librarian for assistance.

As mentioned previously, not all sources will have all of these elements. Figure out what type of source you have by looking through the models listed below and then collect all necessary information. Your reference list must provide the information necessary for a reader to locate and retrieve any source you cite in the body of the paper. Each source you cite in the paper must appear in your reference list; likewise, each entry in the reference list must be cited in your text.

Formatting your citations

List all the sources you use on a separate page or pages (as necessary), titled **References**, with that word centered at the top of the page. (Do *not* bold, underline, or use quotation marks for the title). All text should be double-spaced just like the rest of your essay. The first line of an entry is flush with the left margin, and all subsequent lines of an entry are indented a half-inch from the margin. APA specifies that you spell out months of three or four letters, abbreviating all others to three letters (e.g., June, Dec., Oct.)

For a detailed discussion of all citation models, please refer to the most recent edition of the *APA Publication Manual* or to a handbook that draws on the most recent edition. We cover here models for electronic sources most frequently used in social science and scientific research.

1. Website (home page)

A document from a website with institutional or corporate sponsor

> Attention Deficit Hyperactivity Disorder (ADHD).
>
> (2011, July 5). *The National Institute of Mental Health*. Retrieved from http://www.nimh.nih.gov /health/topics/attention-deficit-hyperactivity -disorder-adhd/index.shtml.

2. Online encyclopedia article

> Griffith, D.A. (2009). Spatial Autocorrelation. The International Encyclopedia of Human Geography. Ed. R. Kitchen and N. Thrift. St. Louis: Elsevier. 1-10. Retrieved from http://www.elsevierdirect .com/brochures/hugy/SampleContent/Spatial -Autocorrelation.pdf.

3. Wiki entry

> Representational momentum. (2011, July 17). Retrieved July 22 from http://en.wikipedia.org/wiki /Representational_momentum.

4. Articles from journals

Article from print journal, found online

> Ditlea, S. (2001). The electronic paper chase. *Scientific American*. Retrieved July 18, 2011, from https://services.brics.dk/java/courseadmin/AR /documents/getDocument/AR-nr29-Ditlea.pdf?d=34192.

From an electronic-only journal

> Aydeniz, M. (2002). Measuring the Impact of Electric
>
> Circuits KitBook on Elementary School Children's
>
> Understanding of Simple Electric Circuits.
>
> *Electronic Journal of Science Education.* 14(2),
>
> 1-29. Retrieved from http://ejse.southwestern
>
> .edu/article/view /7304/5622.

5. Government report

> U. S. Department of Commerce. (2010, Aug).
>
> Consolidated Federal Funds Report for Fiscal
>
> Year 2009. Retrieved from http://www.census.gov
>
> /prod/2010pubs/cffr-09.pdf.

6. Online newspaper article

> ADHD result of passive smoking: study. (2011, July
>
> 17) *International Business Times*. U. S. Edition.
>
> Retrieved on 22 July 2011 from http://www.ibtimes
>
> .com/articles/181681 /20110717/adhd-attention
>
> -deficit-disorder-smoking-affects-children-hyper
>
> -activity-harvard-school-study.htm.

7. Online newsletter

> Bees able to recognise human faces? (2010, Feb. 1).
>
> *Science Oxford Online*. Retrieved 22 July 2011
>
> from http://www.scienceoxfordonline.com/bees
>
> -able-to-recognise-human-faces.

8. Posting

Only archived postings to blogs, forums, listservs, and newsgroups should be referenced. If they are not archived, refer to such sources in your paper as "personal communications" and do not include them in the references section.

Blog

> Lopez-Duran, N. (2010, Feb. 24) ADHD medications and
>
> school performance. [Blog]. Retrieved on 22 July
>
> 2011 from http://www.child-psych.org/2010/02/adhd
>
> -medications-and-school-performance.html.

Forum

> SFOS. (2009, Nov 30). The controversy facing the
>
> Yanomami people. [Message posted to the Anthropol-
>
> ogy Message Board]. Retrieved on 20 July 2011
>
> from http://anthropology.yuku.com/topic/428/the
>
> -controversy-facing-the-Yanomami-peoples.

9. Email message

Generally, avoid including email messages in a list of references and instead cite email in your paper only as personal communication.

10. Podcast

> Flato, I. [Producer]. (2011, July 22). Remodeling
>
> hearts with stem cells. [Audio Podcast].
>
> National Public Radio. Retrieved from
>
> http://www.sciencefriday.com /program
>
> /archives/201107221.

Integrating source materials

When using APA format, you want to follow the author-date method of in-text citation. This means that the author's last name and the year of publication for the source should appear in the text, for example, (`Jones, 1998`), and a complete reference should appear in the reference list at the end of the paper.

Generally in social science and scientific research, no page reference is necessary, but when you are referencing a specific part of a source in your paper, always mention the page, chapter, or table in your citation on the reference page, as well as provide page numbers for any quoted material: (`Smith, 2004, p. 25`); (`Alvarez, 1998, chap. 5`). If you are using a PDF file, you can provide the relevant page references. Many electronic sources, however, do not have page numbers; in this instance, use a paragraph number if given: (`Frankel, 1997, para. 6-9`). In cases when neither page number nor paragraph number is available, refer to the nearest heading and the number of the paragraph following it, which will direct the reader to your source, as in (`Brawley, 1988, see section 2.40`).

Getting additional help

This chapter has provided a general guide to citing electronic sources. We must note that any and all guides to citing inevitably fall behind the exploding new and different genres of web publication. At some point, you will want to use a source for which you cannot find an exact citation model in MLA, APA, Chicago style, or whatever other citation format you are required to use. You should ask your professor for a model in these cases. If you are unable to check with the professor, find the closest possible model and follow it.

7

PRESENTING YOUR WORK ONLINE

Whether you're making a comment on a blog, a post in a forum, or designing an online database of photos and videos, you want the materials you create to look good. Blogs, forums, and wikis now use templates, which means you don't have to understand all the coding that makes the site work, but having a basic understanding of what goes in to making an online document can make your work clearer, easier to use, and better looking.

HTML

HTML, or Hypertext Markup Language, is a set of commands that forms the basis for formatting many web pages. It's also used for blog comments, forum posts, and other places where you can add input without creating an entire website. You need only know a little about HTML in order to share your ideas with billions of web users worldwide. In addition, many other formatting systems use HTML as a basis, so once you have the basics of HTML down, you can easily learn how to use these other systems.

All HTML elements consist of **tags**, which are instructions surrounded in **angle brackets** (< and >). Most elements include an opening and a closing tag. Closing tags are distinguished by a slash mark. So, for example, to make the word **hello** appear in boldface, you'd type: `<b>hello</b>`.

Font styles

`<b>` . . . `</b>`	**Bold-face text**
`<i>` . . . `</i>`	*Italicized text*
`<u>` . . . `</u>`	<u>Underlined text</u>
`<strike>` . . . `</strike>`	~~Strike-through text~~
`<sup>` . . . `</sup>`	Superscript text
`<sub>` . . . `</sub>`	Subscript text

Links

The most common is the link to a document or file:

```
<A HREF="complete address of the file">text you
want people to click on</A>
```

So, for example, if you want to link to the article, "On Not Being Able to Write about Hamlet," you would use the following command:

```
<a href="http://www.clas.ufl.edu/ipsa
/journal/2000_greenberg03.shtml">Here's an
interesting article on Hamlet</a>.
```

Readers would see the text, "Here's an interesting article on Hamlet" and clicking on the text would take them to the article.

You can also link to a sound, graphic, or video file by specifying the proper file name in the link information.

Inline images

Inline images are graphics that are incorporated into the layout of an online document, post, or comment. To place an image into your text, select the point in the document where the image should appear and use the appropriate command. Make sure you enter the complete URL (beginning with *http://*) for the image file.

```
<img src="URL/imagefilename.gif">
```

How do you find the URL of the image? Right-click on it in your browser and select "Copy image URL" or "Copy image address."

If the image is on your computer, you'll first need to upload it to an image service. (See "A quick guide to putting your images online.")

Other formats

Other forums and blogs may use slightly different markup from HTML code. Usually, they will provide links to a help file, or they may also include buttons that can be used to automatically format your comments or posts. Wikis have an entirely different way of formatting entries. For more on formatting wikis, see *en.wikipedia.org/wiki/Wikipedia:How_to_edit_a_page*.

A quick guide to putting your images online

While it's beyond the scope of this text to discuss the technical aspects of image creation, we can offer a few pointers:

- Keep images as small as possible. Some users may have small monitors: 1024 x 768 <u>pixels</u> is most common, and many monitors offer only 800 x 600. That means your images should probably be no more than 600 pixels wide.
- Use Photoshop or another application to reduce your image to the size you need before uploading. Don't just use your camera's default image size, which can be 2592 x 1944 or larger, and might take hours for users to download.
- Some forums limit the size of images you upload to a particular size: 80 kB is a common size. In Photoshop, you can use the "Save for web" command, and adjust the image size and quality until it fits within these restrictions.
- Give the image a name you'll remember, and note the folder where you save it.
- Since images take time to download, make sure they are relevant to your discussion.
- On the other hand, don't skimp on images. Users will quickly tire of page after page of text.

When you're ready to upload your image, follow the instructions on your forum or blog for uploading images. If the site doesn't allow images, you can use a separate service like *flickr.com* or *imageshack.us/* to host the images. Then just link the image from your blog or forum post.

GLOSSARY

Algorithm A system used by a computer application to generate and organize results. In the case of search engines, algorithms are used to organize the results of searches in the way that is most useful to users.

angle bracket (>) 1. Used to denote a reply quotation in email messages. 2. Used in pairs to surround HTML tags.

blog A website with posts arranged in reverse-chronological order, often as a personal record of websites or blogs visited.

blogosphere The global community formed by bloggers and blogs.

bookmark See *favorites*.

Boolean Logical search operators that allow a user to refine the scope of keyword searches. The simple Boolean operators are *and*, *or*, and *not*.

browser A program that allows users to view pages on the web. The four most popular browsers are Microsoft Internet Explorer, Google Chrome, Apple Safari, and Mozilla Firefox.

course management system A website that allows teachers to post course materials, enable class discussions, post grades, and conduct other class business.

Creative Commons licenses A set of easy-to-use open content licenses available at *creativecommons.org*.

Digital Object Identifier (DOI) A unique number corresponding to a specific item stored online. Even if the URL for the item changes, the DOI remains the same; it's a permanent way of finding an online resource. Frequently used for science journal articles and figures. Here is an example DOI: 10.1016/j.compedu.2010.03.012.

directory A subdivision in a computer file system (known as a *folder* in some operating systems). Directories can contain files, applications, or other directories.

domain An element of an Internet or email address specified by an organization or suborganization on the Internet (e.g., *netscape.com, davidson.edu*).

dynamic source Research information that is easily or frequently changed, such as blogs, forums, and wikis.

export To save a file in a different format; often used for creating web pages with a word processor.

e-zine A magazine distributed solely by electronic means, usually in the form of a website.

FAQ (Frequently Asked Questions) A document that collects and responds to some of the most common questions about a particular aspect of the Internet or about a particular topic.

favorites A set of electronic pointers to Internet sites that can be recalled for future reference. Also known as *bookmarks*.

feed See *RSS*.

forum A discussion website where members can post threads organized by topic.

helper application Software that works with an Internet application (such as a browser) to add additional features (such as the capability to listen to real-time audio).

history A list of sites recently visited; often automatically maintained by your web browser.

HTML (Hypertext Markup Language) A scripting language used to turn plain text and other elements (such as images) into the integrated pages pictured on the web.

keyword 1. A word or group of words used in an electronic search to locate documents about a particular topic. 2. A descriptive word or group of words specified by the author or indexer of a document to facilitate electronic searches.

literal search A search for an exact phrase or grouping of words, usually indicated with quotation marks.

MPEG (pronounced *EM-peg*) A video format often used on the web.

netiquette A set of rules for behavior on the Internet, usually dictated by convenience and common sense.

open content or **open source** Material that authors have agreed to let others use for free, subject to restrictions they specify.

paraphrase To express someone else's idea in your own words.

PDF (Portable Document Format) An electronic format often used for online versions of printed documents. The formatting and page numbers of the original are preserved.

pixel A single dot, or element, of a picture. Image sizes on the web are measured in pixels.

plagiarism Intentionally or accidentally presenting someone else's work as one's own. A serious offense that can be grounds for failing a course or expulsion.

plug-in See *helper application.*

robot See *search engine.*

RSS A regularly updated feed of information from a website or database. You can subscribe to any RSS feed using a reader such as Google Reader, and you'll automatically receive updates or even get notified via email.

scholarly database A searchable index of articles and other documents created and reviewed by experts in their field (e.g., PsychInfo and Web of Knowledge).

search engine A program usually accessed via a website that allows users to perform keyword searches on the Internet (e.g., Google, Bing).

social media site A site like Facebook or Twitter that allows people to easily post personal information and connect with others.

spam 1. Email sent to large numbers of recipients without their first requesting it. 2. Postings of irrelevant messages to newsgroups or listservs. 3. Any attempt to push unwanted information on Internet users by making use of repetitious computing power.

static source Research information that is created once and generally unchanged thereafter. Includes most printed material, plus online resources like PDFs, videos, and scholarly journals.

subject directory A directory of services on the Internet organized hierarchically.

tag 1. A keyword assigned by the author to an online research to make it easier for others to find. 2. An instruction in HTML or another markup style.

uploading Placing a file or application on a remote host over the Internet. Often used to put text, sound, graphics, video, and HTML files on a web server for publication.

URL (Uniform Resource Locator) The address assigned to each document on the Internet. Consists of the protocol, followed by two slashes, the domain name and type, the directory path, and the file name.

virus A computer program designed to spread from computer to computer, in a manner analogous to the way a biological virus spreads among living organisms. Most electronic viruses are now transmitted via email attachments. While many viruses are benign, others can cause significant damage by destroying files or disabling programs. Even more troubling is the fact that, unlike natural viruses, computer viruses are created by people. It is our sincere hope that a special place in hell is reserved for virus programmers.

web browser See *browser.*

wiki A website that any user can change.

For more information about computer terms, visit the Free On-Line Dictionary of Computing at *foldoc.org/.*

CREDITS

CHAPTER 1

Figure 1.1, Google search for "political polarization." Google is a trademark of Google Inc.

Figure 1.2, Google search for "political polarization and the Internet." Google is a trademark of Google Inc.

CHAPTER 2

Figure 2.1, Google search for "Hamlet." Google is a trademark of Google Inc.

Figure 2.2, Google search for "political polarization and social media." Google is a trademark of Google Inc.

Figure 2.3, Google search for "political polarization and social media" using –. Google is a trademark of Google Inc.

Figure 2.4, Google search for "political polarization" using + and –. Google is a trademark of Google Inc.

Figure 2.5, Google advanced search. Google is a trademark of Google Inc.

Figure 2.6, Google advanced search – *Wikipedia*. Google is a trademark of Google Inc.

Figure 2.7, The Child Psychology page on Open Directory. This work is licensed under a Creative Commons Attribution 3.0 Unported License, www.dmoz.org/license.html.

Figure 2.8, Google search for "ADHD." Google is a trademark of Google Inc.

Figure 2.9, Google Scholar search for "ADHD." Google is a trademark of Google Inc.

Figure 2.10, A Twitter search for "political polarization." www.twitter.com.

Figure 2.10, Minyanville Tweet, July 8, 2011. Tweet by permission of Kevin Depew, Minyanville Media, Inc.

Figure 2.10, JPie612 Tweet, July 6, 2011. Reprinted by permission.

Figure 2.10, Ziggy_Daddy Tweet, July 5, 2011. Reprinted by permission.

Figure 2.10, Two VoteSmartToday Tweets, July 5, 2011 by Richard D. Cushing. Reprinted by permission.

Figure 2.11, A Research Blogging search for "ADHD." Reprinted by permission of ResearchBlogging.org.

CHAPTER 3

Figure 3.1, Google Scholar search showing citations. Google is a trademark of Google Inc.

Figure 3.2, Science-Based Medicine website. From www.sciencebasedmedicine.org. Reprinted by permission.

CHAPTER 4

Figure 4.1, Screen capture from PubMed using Zotero to track information. www.zotero.org.

INDEX